T

ALSO WRITTEN BY JILL RAPPAPORT AND WENDY WILKINSON
PHOTOGRAPHY BY LINDA SOLOMON

People We Know, Horses They Love

Mazel Tov

Celebrities' Bar and Bat Mitzvah Memories

Written by
Jill Rappaport

Photography by
Linda Solomon

SIMON & SCHUSTER
New York   London   Toronto   Sydney

SIMON & SCHUSTER
Rockefeller Center
1230 Avenue of the Americas
New York, NY 10020

First Simon & Schuster hardcover edition October 2007

SIMON & SCHUSTER and colophon are registered trademarks
of Simon & Schuster, Inc.

For information about special discounts for bulk purchases, please contact Simon &
Schuster Special Sales at 1-800-456-6798 or business@simonandschuster.com

Manufactured in China

10 9 8 7 6 5 4 3 2 1

Library of Congress Cataloging-in-Publication Data

Rappaport, Jill.
Mazel tov: celebrities' bar and bat mitzvahs / Jill Rappaport and Linda Solomon.
p. cm.
1. Bar mitzvah—Anecdotes.   2. Bat mitzvah—Anecdotes.   3. Celebrities—Anecdotes.
4. Celebrities—Interviews.   5. Celebrities—Biography.   6. Jews—Anecdotes.   7. Jews—
Interviews.   8. Jews—Biography.   I. Solomon, Linda (Linda Rappaport) II. Title.

BM707.R37 2007
296.4'4240922—dc22

2007007916

ISBN-13: 978-0-7432-8787-6
ISBN-10:   0-7432-8787-8

ACKNOWLEDGMENTS

First and foremost we would like to thank Kate Marcus, whose hard work, talent, dedication and passion for this project made the book possible.

A heartfelt thank you to all of the wonderful people we worked with at Simon & Schuster including our outstanding editor, Amanda Murray; her incredible assistant, Annie Orr; and the always supportive David Rosenthal. We also would like to personally thank Michael Korda for his enthusiasm and interest right from the inception of the book.

Also, special thanks to Katie Hockmeyer, Lindsay King, Katie Murphy, Bridget Leininger, Joyce Piven, Stacy Green, Billy Daley, Devin Johnson, Sabrina Clay, Guy Ludwig, Christine Taylor, Ashley Stachowski, Rich Thurber, Nicki Fioravante, Rose Snyder, Leslie Adler, Stephanie Jones, Mary Duffy, Erika Masonhall, Marshall Wittman, Jessica Michaels, Marla Kleiner, Jack Jason, Jody Smith, Mary Garrigan, Tarik Flannagan, Andrea Smith, Lisa Kussell, Jon Streep, Jill Fritzo, Ron Fierstein, Donna Bojarsky, Diane Harrington, Julie Nathanson and Amos Remer.

CONTENTS

Mazel Tov

INTRODUCTION
By Jill Rappaport

You might be asking, What's a nice Jewish girl from Michigan doing writing a book about the bar and bat mitzvah experience when I never had one myself? Well, because I did. . . . Even though I personally never got to utter those precious words, "Today I am a Wo-Man," the bat mitzvah experience left an indelible mark on my life, and here's why: at thirteen, no one loved a party more than I. And boy, those were some *serious* celebrations intensified by my *serious* crushes on some of the boys. The service seemed to give these thirteen-year-olds an air of confidence that they did not have the day before. Maybe that phrase "Today I am a Man" is more poignant than we think. However, being the *deep* thirteen-year-old that I was, the stellar moments for me included the excitement of wondering what to wear, putting on way too much makeup, then parading into the parties with my best pals, Lisa Lapides and Laurie Dean, and watching the boys check us out. I should mention I dreaded the hora but kicked butt in the bunny hop.

As for my childhood, I was born in Detroit and raised in a Reform home. My wonderful, supportive, and nurturing parents, Mona and Daniel Rappaport, were not very religious, but respected the Jewish tradition and passed that on to my sister, Linda, and me. When I was ten, we moved to Bloomfield Hills but continued to go to Temple Israel in Detroit. To be honest, I dreaded Sunday school, and the idea of memorizing all the Hebrew required to be bat mitzvahed was not exactly my idea of a good time. So, fortunately, my parents gave me another option: confirmation. Again, the weekly classes were a nightmare, but the final celebration, the party, was fabulous! Deep, huh? I realized at that moment that what I had done was special. I was blessed to have gone through the ritual. The year was_____. (I can't say; my mother does not allow me to reveal my age.) But I can say the month: it was June. Of course I remember what I wore; you never forget the important things in life. And what an outfit it was. . . . Can you say *frightening?!* We're talking a shiny, floral, one-piece, sleeveless hot pants number with a wraparound skirt open in the front to expose my gams. This was definitely a fashion "Don't," but I "Did" it anyway, and the scary thing is that I thought I looked fabulous. So did my boyfriend at the time, Steve Finkel. But what did he know? His hair was longer than mine, and he wore a corduroy jacket with velour pants. Mr. Blackwell would have *kvelled. That* list I would have made! . . . The celebration after the service was at our home. Everyone came to pay homage to me, the girl who was voted "Most Seen in the Halls Without a Pass" in high school. Needless to say, I was every teacher's

JILL RAPPAPORT (LEFT) AND FRIENDS

worst nightmare, and I did not fare much better with the rabbi. They all used to shake their heads and say, "God help your parents."

That said, I was lucky to have Rabbi M. Robert Syme in my life. He was a warm and dear man whose expressions have stayed with me throughout my life—for example, "Every day, God gives you twenty-four gold coins, and it is up to you how you spend them." The idea that every hour of every day is precious is something that I try to remember. He was a very special person.

Looking back, my confirmation was a significant moment in my life and an important milestone. Fast forward: years later. . . . (Don't worry, Mom, I won't say how many.) And here's the book, featuring special bar and bat mitzvah memories. I even threw in a confirmation, and I would like to say I hope you find the stories shared by these many wonderful, well-known people to be as touching, heartfelt, and hilarious as I did. In talking with each individual about his or her own experience as a Jewish thirteen-year-old in the limelight, it was clear that each was affected in a profound way. Some knew they were born to be on stage or in front of a camera, like CNN's talk guru, Larry King, and Emmy-winner Jeremy Piven. Others discovered they could have the power to lead, like NBC's president and chief executive officer, Jeff Zucker, and U.S. Senator Joseph Lieberman. A few overcame tremendous difficulties to even have a bar or bat mitzvah, like Oscar-winner Marlee Matlin and actor Henry Winkler. And one decided the bar mitzvah experience was even more special the second time around . . . even at eighty-three years old, says beloved actor Kirk Douglas. From doing it *his way,* like designer Michael Kors, to having *no say,* like *Deal or No Deal* host Howie Mandel. Every story is unique and heartfelt, and the fact that this book focuses not only on bar mitzvahs, but also bat mitzvahs, and even confirmations, makes it that much more interesting. You will see that all recognize their celebration as a significant and enlightening rite of passage. Despite some humiliating moments for a few, this was the point at which they were launched into the world as responsible people. And *Mazel tov!* for making it part of your library. Maybe after reading this book, you will say, "Today I am a *fan!!*"

Linda Solomon

The phone rang, and it was my best friend in elementary school, Michelle Nickin, screaming with excitement, "Did you get the invitation?" With great disappointment, I had to answer "No." The mail hadn't arrived. I decided to wait on the sidewalk. After minutes that seemed like hours, I finally spotted our mailman. He was smiling and waving a parchment envelope bearing my name, elegantly engraved by a calligrapher. It was The Invitation . . . my first invitation to a friend's bar mitzvah. I remember every detail about Bobby Fleisher's special day. It was so very special for me too. From this day on, I saved every bar mitzvah invitation I had received and kept them in order with Bobby's on top. My mother made a beautiful floral box for me, and I placed each invitation in this box and safely stored them under the window seat in my bedroom. My mother still lives in the house where Jill and I grew up. Not too long ago, I was looking for some things in my bedroom. It looks exactly the way it did when I was thirteen. I decided to open the window seat, and there was the floral box. Bobby's invitation was still on top.

When I was fourteen I began to prepare for my confirmation at Temple Israel in Detroit. Our grandparents, Elisabeth (Bess) and Louis Rappaport, were founding members of our temple. Temple Israel on Manderson Road was so very elegant and beautiful with its mahogany walls and marble foyer. The year our class was confirmed, stained glass windows depicting our Jewish heritage were created for the temple. Each member of my confirmation class was asked to memorize a passage that described a story from one of the windows. My portion (four lines) referred to the window describing the life of Rabbi Leo Beck. Recently, one of my friends who was in my confirmation class told me he still remembered my four lines, since all I did every day for months was repeat every single word in those four lines to anyone who would listen. The thought of speaking in front of the congregation made me very nervous. I have to admit and I am embarrassed to reveal that I did walk up to the *bima* with my four lines written on my hand just in case. My parents celebrated my confirmation with our family and close friends at a beautiful afternoon luncheon at our house. It was a sunny June day, picture perfect, and I was the photographer so I'm not in many of the photographs. I used my Polaroid Swinger, one of my confirmation gifts, to capture my special day.

It has been many years since my confirmation. Every year at the high holy days, I reflect back. Temple Israel has relocated and is a much larger and contemporary synagogue, but the beautiful eternal light from the original temple remains eternal. And the stained glass windows designed and created during my confirmation class still adorn, and the bright and beautiful colors of the image in the Leo Beck window reflect my history.

Linda Solomon (center) at her confirmation luncheon

Jeremy Piven

As the son of two acting teachers, Jeremy Piven certainly had great footsteps to follow in and his stellar career speaks for itself. With close to fifty film credits under his belt, plus an Emmy for Best Supporting Actor in a comedy, playing Agent Ari Gold in HBO's *Entourage,* Piven, known for his scene stealing roles, is truly on a roll himself.

Born on July 26, 1965, to Byrne and Joyce Hiller Piven, acting was in his blood long before his bar mitzvah. Byrne and Joyce studied acting, and in 1967, the entourage, including Byrne and Joyce, Jeremy, and his older sister, Shira, relocated to Chicago from New York. In Chicago the Pivens founded the Piven Theatre Workshop. At eight, Jeremy had his first acting job in his parents' theater, doing Chekhov. He graduated from Evanston Township High School, where he played football, and attended Drake University in Des Moines, Iowa, and the Tisch School of the Arts at New York University.

At the age of nine, he befriended John Cusack, who, with his sister, Joan, was a student at the Piven Theatre Workshop. Years later, Piven and Cusack founded New Crime Productions, which can take credit for *Grosse Pointe Blank* and *High Fidelity.* Among his dozens of films are *Lucas, The Player, Bob Roberts, Singles, Miami Rhapsody,* and *Old School,* and *Keeping Up with the Steins,* which is about one-upsmanship in the bar mitzvah world. Piven displayed his ability to rap in Hebrew in the 2004 film *Chasing Liberty.* He was in a variety of television shows, beginning with *Carol & Company* and continuing in programs such as *The Larry Sanders Show, Ellen, Seinfeld,* and *Entourage.*

At thirteen Jeremy Piven celebrated his bar mitzvah, in a wholly unlikely location.

JOYCE PIVEN WITH HER SON, JEREMY

I was bar mitzvahed in Evanston, Illinois, in a church because we were a very liberal congregation of Reform Jews, called Reconstructionists. My father used to joke that we prayed to To Whom It May Concern.

Besides the studying part, I helped prepare for the event by drawing the picture on the invitation, which was so much fun. I drew pictures of the band KISS and I drew things that I loved from inside the Torah. My parents structured the day. The ceremony was modest but I think there were about two hundred people there. Only about forty were my friends. The rest was family. My parents read poetry, and because they're real artists, it was a pretty cool bar mitzvah. We didn't have a band but afterwards there was dancing in my basement. I put on my records. I wanted to honor the occasion in my own way. I didn't really have any reverence for the big party. It wasn't a big community of people battling each other for the biggest bar mitzvah, like in my movie *Keeping Up with the Steins*.

I had no desire for the big fancy party. And we were a theater family living in Evanston. It was just a way of gathering my friends together, and to take part in the tradition that my father had passed down to me. My friends showed up. I didn't really have a girlfriend at the time, but a girl that I liked showed up. And I think it was a real novelty to them, because it was one of the only bar mitzvahs going. For the most part, my friends had not been to one. So it was a new experience and they loved it.

But being thirteen wasn't only about the bar mitzvah. At the time, I was also playing football. That was a real focal point of my life. My team actually would win quite a bit, and after a game, the team would go to McDonald's to celebrate. Instead of going to McDonald's, my father took me, one of the very few white kids on the team, to Hebrew school. So, unfortunately, my Jewishness was introduced in a negative way, but in time I grew to appreciate it all.

Turning thirteen and being bar mitzvahed is a rite of passage. We all need rites of passage and markings of times and all these things. And it meant a lot to my father. So at the time it may have been even more about him than me, and what a beautiful thing for him to pass on to me. My father was very religious and incredibly active in his community. He was a singer and probably would have been a cantor or a rabbi had he not been an actor. He was very connected to his Judaism.

You have to understand that from the time I was eight years old, my parents were putting me up on the stage. I was working with them. And I was in classes and doing improv, and so I was always acting with them, and that was our temple, in a way. But I never got ahead of myself and thought, Well, this is what I'm going to be doing for the rest of my life.

YOU CAME FROM A VERY INTERESTING BACKGROUND. WERE YOU ALWAYS THE CENTER OF ATTENTION?

I guess I was kind of popular back then. My mother, or my sister, probably would've said I was. I do like to laugh and I like to make other people laugh. Definitely, my parents said I was jumping up and landing on my side to get people to laugh very early on.

JEREMY WITH FRIENDS LAUREN KATZ (LEFT) AND ANNA SHAPIRO

DO I DARE ASK—WHAT DID YOU LOOK LIKE BACK THEN?

I had a big chubby bar mitzvah boy face and what was bordering on a mullet. I liked the suit. The suit looked great. It was a pinstriped, three-piece suit with the big, wide white collar. I was very into *Saturday Night Fever.* I remember seeing a picture with John Travolta behind me, from *Saturday Night Fever.* I was holding an album of Parliament and the P-Funk All-Stars, with Bootsy Collins and George Clinton and everyone. It was a beautiful, wonderful time. I'll never forget it.

And looking back, I can't help but think how lucky I was to have this really loving, cool, artistic family. We just didn't have a lot of money, but if you don't miss it, who cares? And I mean that.

YOUR FILM, *KEEPING UP WITH THE STEINS,* SHEDS QUITE A LIGHT ON THE BAR MITZVAH EXPERIENCE, BUT IT WAS THE COMPLETE OPPOSITE OF YOUR OWN BLESSED EVENT.

Oh yeah, well completely. That's why I thought it was really interesting, because I learned that this world exists: people getting these rap stars to come to their bar mitzvahs and more. It's just so right for comedy, a world that I didn't experience, but thought it would be so funny to explore. And so I had a blast, but it was quite different than my experience. The movie is about forgiveness and connection and love in this family, but to get there you have to go through a bunch of dysfunctional people.

YOU ARE SINGLE, NO KIDS YET, BUT IF YOU HAD A SON, WOULD YOU WANT HIM TO BE BAR MITZVAHED?

It would be great. It would be a completely amazing gift.

Byrne Piven with his son, Jeremy

13

Michael Kors

Fashion icon Michael Kors was born in 1959 and grew up on Long Island, not far from New York City, where he would become a leading designer of women's and men's clothing (he is now called "King Kors"). From the beginning Kors had a keen sense of design and was completely obsessed by how the world around him looked. His bar mitzvah stands out as his first opportunity to create the look of a big celebration, from top to toe. His parents were happy to have the input. His mother was one of his first teachers in the art of design and he went on to attend the Fashion Institute of Technology.

Just six years after his bar mitzvah, when he was nineteen, Kors was designing for the New York boutique, Lothar's. In 1981, he launched his own women's wear line, which sold in Saks Fifth Avenue and Bloomingdales and other stores. He introduced a signature fragrance for women in 2000. He launched his men's fragrance in 2001, and then in 2002, he created his extensive menswear line, which grew from a small collection he started in 1997. In 2004, Michael Kor's newest collection, MICHAEL, was launched in over three hundred fifty locations. This collection offers women's ready-to-wear, swimwear and a complete line of accessories including handbags, shoes, watches, eyewear, and belts.

Fans of clothing by Kors include Madonna, Jennifer Lopez, Barbra Streisand, Sharon Stone, Pierce Brosnan and Rene Russo, whose wardrobe Kors produced for the 1999 remake of *The Thomas Crown Affair*. Besides making clothes that make the woman and the man, Kors also became a television personality, as an "underwhelmed" judge on *Project Runway*.

After being bar mitzvahed, Michael Kors went on to receive many other honors. Vogue anointed him one of the most influential designers of the decade in 1996. Three years later, he was awarded the Council of Fashion Designers of America (CFDA) Award for Womenswear Designer of the Year, and Lighthouse International honored him with the Lifetime Achievement Award. In 2003, he won the CFDA Menswear Award.

MICHAEL KORS, DESIGNING KID

I was always a fashion freak. My mother and I turned the whole arranging of my bar mitzvah into a year and a half of "What's the matchbook look like, what's the invitation look like, what's the centerpiece, what are you wearing? Who's wearing what, when, how?" So, of course, I loved all that. My personal theme was blue for the day and brown at night. The invitation, it was all mustard and chocolate brown. Mustard envelopes, mustard matches. It was the seventies. Mustard was a basic.

My bar mitzvah was not typical. When people called my mom and said, "What should I wear?" my mother said, "Wear whatever you want. If you want to wear a gown, wear a gown. If you want to wear jeans, wear jeans. If you want to wear a bikini, wear a bikini." So my parents had a lot of friends who were full hippie-dippie. And they all came in gauze and embroidered jeans, riding on motorcycles.

And then my uncle wore a leather jacket and shirt unbuttoned to his waist. And my aunt wore a bikini top and matching cotton pants. I didn't come from the normal family. Everyone was young; my mom had me young. It was the counterculture bar mitzvah.

My Jewish relatives all came in evening gowns, even though it was outside and supposedly casual on the water. My Episcopalian relatives all came as though they were going to the country club in navy blazers and white pants. So we had this strange convergence. All of my friends' mothers were totally perplexed. "He can wear jeans?" And my mom said, "He can wear whatever he wants."

I was the fashion designer back then, full tilt. I'm an only child so, for my mom, the event was really exciting. And she always trusted my judgment. My grandmother kept telling her, "You can't let a twelve-year-old decide on the dinner menu." But she did to a certain extent.

My bar mitzvah would've been more off the wall, actually, if my mother had let me really go for it. I wanted to serve fondue. The idea nearly gave my grandmother a heart attack. My grandmother: "It's June. It's hot. They're Jewish people. They're not eating hot cheese on a piece of bread for dinner." In my defense, fondue and quiche were very trendy at the moment. It was that time of ferns in a hanging basket, fondue and quiche.

Even back when I grew up, the bar mitzvahs were way over the top, and thematic. There was always a theme, a crazy theme. Mine wasn't over the top, but it was different. It was in a tent on the water. It was low key. We had two bands, a classic bar mitzvah band,

Joan Kors with her son, Michael

which played "Hava Nagila" and all of that, and then we had a folksinging couple from Vermont, Dick and Georgia. And when they started singing, you could see that all the Jewish relatives were thinking: "Who the hell are they?" I loved that.

No. I was a performer. I've always been a performer. That wasn't the problem. I *was* scared I'd mess up. But I loved the whole process of getting bar mitzvahed. It's funny, when I got bar mitzvahed in the 1970s on Long Island, it was bar mitzvah madness. The synagogues couldn't even manage to give you your own date. So two boys got bar mitzvahed at the same time. I was bar mitzvahed with another boy, named Mitchell Tansmen, who I later saw at my high school reunion. He was nice but he was very studious and very serious. And he was very nervous. And his parents were sort of straight and narrow. His mother was head of the sisterhood, and his father was part of the young men's association. My mom was in a minidress and my dad had long hair, it was longer than my mother's, and he had a handlebar mustache. We were the alternative bar mitzvah family.

This will sound so incredibly shallow, but I was truly style and shopping obsessed. Our family had friends who were just the WASP-iest people on the planet, who had never been to a bar mitzvah, and really did not know that you basically give a check or a cash gift. When I was in front of the crowd, I saw the friends in the back of the temple. And I was sitting waiting to go up and do my haftarah. They had an enormous brown-and-white-striped Bendel box sitting with them. And all I could think of was, What's in the box? I wanted to get over this whole haftarah moment, and let's just find out what's in the Bendel box. I think my grandfather said something about the gift not being in an envelope. But I didn't want the cash. I wanted the Bendel box. At that point in my life I was obsessed. I was doing a makeover on every person I ever met.

I didn't wake up that morning and suddenly think, Oh, my God, I'm going to be an adult, a man overnight. But I do think that in a quieter way, my bar mitzvah did let me know that, as an adult, your opinions really do count. Your actions count as an adult. It is your adult introduction to some of these people, people your parents do business with or whatever. It is your first adult moment. So I think that it has impact. The bar mitzvah is such a big deal. It was funny, in the days before my bar mitzvah, we had semihurricanes all week. So it rained every day. It was horrible. Endless rain, endless rain, endless rain. I thought the dance floor would sink into the mud. And the morning of my bar mitzvah, I woke up and it was sunny and beautiful. And I thought, Maybe there is something to all this. And you know the dance floor still sunk, actually.

A large party, a tiny party, whether you had a thousand people or you had twenty people, it doesn't matter. For me it was exciting just to have everyone around who was important to me: my family, my friends, everyone, my neighbors, all gathered together honoring this momentous day. Who knew I would do this? I was, quite honestly, terrible in Hebrew school. I was never really good in any school, to be honest with you. But in Hebrew school, specifically, I was not a great student. I was really more interested in going home and seeing *Dark Shadows* on television or watching *The Mike Douglas Show* rather than going to my Hebrew lessons. So I do remember being scared over my lack of preparation about a month before my bar mitzvah.

My mother was, like, "So, how are you doing?" And I'm like, "Good." And my mother's saying, "Do you want to recite a little for me?" And at this point I could recite maybe two lines which I had memorized. I didn't learn how to read Hebrew. And I guess it's in moments like this that it was good that my father's family is not Jewish. They had no idea that my pronunciation wasn't perfect. I think I was their first bar mitzvah, so it was news to them. Meanwhile, there were my other grandparents; my grandmother was rolling her eyes at my phonetic pronunciations.

NOW WHAT LEFT MORE OF AN IMPRESSION ON YOU: THE SERVICE OR THE PARTY?

I think I knew the sentimental value but the religious value, honestly, no. We were beyond Reform Jews. I mean, here we were: "Thank you so much for coming, have a glass of wine." I have wonderful Jewish prince memories of the two things that I'm so fortunate to have experienced: the years of sleepaway camp and a bar mitzvah. Because I mean, especially on Long Island, if you didn't have a bar mitzvah, you'd want to have one, even if you were an Irish Catholic. You had to have one. Now people do have bar mitzvahs for non-Jewish children. That's the trend in New York now.

Well it was a toss-up between show business and fashion. And let's be honest. Fashion is show business. It's all the same. When I think about what I was like when I was twelve, I certainly picked the right thing. Because, as I said, I was obsessed with every detail.

My parents totally loved it. I mean, loved it. My mother and my grandmother never saw eye to eye on fashion. They always were like Endora and Samantha on *Bewitched* when it came to fashion. And my grandparents wore matching outfits to the synagogue. They wore red, white and blue head to toe. My grandfather wore a red, white and blue tie with a navy blazer and pinstriped pants with a red and navy hat and leather Gucci loafers. Insane. My grandmother wore this crazy navy and white dress with red trim.

I asked my mother to wear spring colors to the bar mitzvah. My grandmother didn't like the dress and told her, "I think it's too much color. You know, you should wear something simpler." And my mother said to my grandmother, "I'm thin enough. I can wear whatever I want. If you were a size four, and five feet eight, this is what you would wear." My grandmother said, "Well, fine. Wear whatever you want." And then my grandmother showed up in this red, white and blue number. My mother whispered to me, "And she thinks that's flattering?" I didn't like the dress either, but I loved my grandfather's shoes. He bought those shoes just for the bar mitzvah.

My friends were dressed in everything and anything. I had a girlfriend, Judy Lerner, who wore a powder blue and white striped cotton jersey gown, like a tank gown, to the floor that was slit up both sides to the waist with matching hot pants and white stockings with the white platform shoes. And she was a head taller than me, of course. I loved the hot pants.

This was about the time when the movie *Goodbye, Columbus* came out. It was my very favorite movie. Brenda Patimkin is my favorite person ever, ever, ever. Brenda Patimkin is the ultimate Jewish girl of all time. When she snapped her bikini bottom . . .

When I think about my bar mitzvah it was something akin to a wedding. It had that kind of excitement and that kind of planning and all that constant back-and-forth. I was overwhelmed. I was not underwhelmed. And then there was the money at the end of it. My mother didn't want me to go wild but she let me decide what to do with it. I wanted an Afghan hound, a dog. So I got one and the rest I banked for college. Of course, as my mother, years later, said, an ivory-colored Afghan hound was not exactly a normal thirteen-year-old boy's dog choice. You know, I thought I was in, like, an art deco movie. Then, right before I left for college, I took some of the money and bought a fabulous wardrobe, and a Cartier watch and a few other things. I was Jappy and proud of it. I am completely proud of it. I do not think it's derogatory at all. And I think it's a plus.

MICHAEL AND PARENTS, BILL AND JOAN KORS

Harvey Fierstein

Provocative, groundbreaking and *hilarious*—three words used to describe Harvey Fierstein, the man with one of the most distinctive voices in the world. The only person in the history of American theater to hold Tony Awards for acting and writing in the dramatic and musical categories, the Brooklyn native also earned his plaque on Brooklyn's Walk of Fame through his work as a playwright, actor, and gay rights activist.

Getting his start as an actor in the 1970s, he was a part of the performance art world in New York. The camp, the drag, the experimental—Harvey pulled it all together. He was a major force in bringing the unapologetic, openly gay life to the public. In 1971, in Andy Warhol's only theatrical production, *Pork,* Fierstein went all out in his role as an asthmatic gay cleaning woman. Fierstein has since worked on the stage in over seventy shows. His *Torch Song Trilogy,* a play and screenplay based on his life that he not only wrote, but starred in, sent his career skyrocketing. He won two Tonys for that show, one for Best Play, the other for Best Actor, and received two Drama Desk Awards, an Obie, and a Dramatists Guild Award. He was awarded another Tony when he wrote the book for the musical *La Cage aux Folles.* In 2003, he was awarded the Tony for Best Performance by a Leading Actor in a Musical for *Hairspray,* in which he wowed audiences with his performance as an endearing two-hundred-fifty-pound mother. Two years later, Harvey Fierstein was back on Broadway as Broadway's favorite father, Tevye, in the musical *Fiddler on the Roof.*

Harvey Fierstein's work in movies has entertained audiences of all ages, again proving his tremendous range as a writer and actor in his adaptation of *Torch Song Trilogy,* in the HBO Showcase *Tidy Endings* and in the Showtime TV movie *Common Ground.* He

has acted in myriad films: *Mrs. Doubtfire, Bullets Over Broadway, Death to Smoochy, Garbo Talks, The Harvest, Dr. Jekyll and Ms. Hyde, Independence Day, Kull the Conquerer, Double Platinum,* and in NBC's *The Year Without a Santa Claus.*

His distinctive gravelly voice has been heard by television audiences in an episode of *The Simpsons,* as Homer's executive secretary, in the Academy Award–winning documentary *The Times of Harvey Milk,* which he narrated. For the HBO special *The Sissy Duckling,* Fierstein created a modem version of the well-known children's story and was the voice of the lead role. The show won a Humanitas Award and was published as a book by Simon & Schuster.

His appearances on television include a recurring role in the sitcom *Cheers* and *Daddy's Girls* with Dudley Moore, and in *Elmo Saves Christmas, Murder She Wrote, Miami Vice, Swellagant Elegance,* and *Those Two,* a CBS pilot.

Harvey Fierstein's massive talents can be heard in the album *This Is Not Going to Be Pretty,* which includes stand-up comedy, dramatic monologues and music.

And when he's not wowing audiences, you can find Harvey doing what he loves most—indulging in his passion for antiques.

HARVEY WITH HIS BROTHER, RON

HARVEY FIERSTEIN
A "TORTURE" SONG TRILOGY

I was always a different kind of a boy. At preschool age I played with dolls. I had a doll carriage. I made dresses for dolls. I was a different kind of a boy. By the time I was thirteen I had skipped two grades in school so I was much less mature than the rest of the kids in my class. There's a big difference between being thirteen years old and fifteen. But at thirteen, only a couple of months after my bar mitzvah, I would be leaving my neighborhood school in Brooklyn and heading to Manhattan to attend the High School of Art and Design. When I hit high school I suddenly exploded from a quiet insular type to a raving maniac. I came out.

The High School of Art and Design was in many ways a gay school. There were a lot of gay kids there. Male and female. Hey, it was an *art* school. Where else would we be? But even back in Bensonhurst a lot of the kids I grew up with, even the really butch ones, turned out to be gay. My mother would tell me, "Oh, I ran into So-and-so and guess what? He's gay! What is it with you all? Was it something in the water?"

ARE YOU A RELIGIOUS PERSON?

I never really believed in God. I always found the concept of some great creator sitting around watching and judging everything every human being did was just silly. And the idea that this all-seeing, all-knowing creator could care about which building and which rituals people used to celebrate creation was the height of human self-centeredness. Anyway, all the Jewish kids I knew attended four years of Hebrew school and then on the day of their bar/ bas mitzvah, they ran as quickly as they could for the secular exit and never looked back. But I did find that religion provided a certain community and identity for me. I definitely viewed myself as Jewish, and then judged others as "tribe members" or not. And in my idealistic teen years I recognized that this sorting of people was destructive.

When I turned thirteen and it was time for my bar mitzvah, I was already looking at religion as a negative force in the world. Still, I did want a bar mitzvah because all my friends had them, and all kids just want to fit in, and I wanted that party . . . and so I got *that party*. The whole affair could qualify as a social disaster. My maternal grandmother, bless her soul, was not an easy lady. What is the name for those people who are totally self-involved . . . ?

That'll do. These were psychologically simpler times. As the only girl in her family, and eight brothers to care for, she seldom had her way. Forced to drop out of school to care for the family, when she finally grew up she rebelled and made *everything* about her. She had quite a flair for the dramatic. I may have her to thank for my career. Anyway, she had to be warned before the bar mitzvah that if she misbehaved by throwing a scene there would be hell to pay. Over the years she'd ruined my uncle's wedding and several other family events so a stern warning was definitely in order. So, with that bit of family history I was bar mitz-vahed at the temple on my block.

The Yeshiva of Bensonhurst stands in Bensonhurst, Brooklyn, on 79th Street between 20th and 21st Avenues. The yeshiva was right down the block from my house. At the other end of the block was the JCH, the Jewish Community House. I was raised Jew-centric. When it came to the holidays I was very jealous that the Christian kids had Christmas trees and all the lights. I wanted to do something fun like that. But Jewish tradition frowned on such goyish displays.

HEY HARVEY, WE DO HAVE PURIM TO CELEBRATE AND YOU GET TO EAT ALL THE PRUNE HAMANTASCHEN YOU WANT.

Yes, and the next morning everyone has a good bowel movement, and that, to a Jew, is a celebration.

So what I did was, I took Glass Wax—remember that pink stuff, that glass cleaner? I took that and food coloring and I mixed up some colored paint and I covered our front windows with Hanukkah designs, lighting them from behind with lamps. This was my own rendition of stained-glass windows. Our rabbi, Rabbi Scharffman, lived farther up the block, so he had to walk by our house on his way to temple every day. Apparently, there was a very serious debate concerning my windows. Several people complained to the temple that this is not the Jewish way. But the rabbi actually stood up for me. He told the people that this was my personal expression of faith and there's absolutely nothing wrong with it. Chagall had just created the windows in the Hadassah Hospital. They were a big thing back then. So he compared my work to the Hadassah windows by Chagall and quelled the controversy. Only I knew there was a core difference between those graphic expressions. Chagall was making art and money. I was making pretty!

Harvey with his parents, Irving and Jacqueline Fierstein,
cousin Shari Gilbert, and brother, Ron

SO YOU ALWAYS EXPRESSED YOURSELF. BUT BACK TO YOUR WACKY GRANDMOTHER.... I'M
ALMOST AFRAID TO ASK: WHAT DID SHE DO AT YOUR BAR MITZVAH?

So there we are at the temple. And this may be hard for you to imagine, but I had a beautiful soprano voice. Before my voice changed, and it had not changed when I was thirteen, I
performed with a professional men's choir that sang on high holy days. I was a boy soprano.
I had one of those voices. In old Italy they would have chopped my balls off and I would've
been a castrato. Anyway, I was looking forward to singing my haftarah, which I'd mastered
beautifully. Before I begin singing I get up on the altar. All of a sudden there's all this com-
motion in the women's section of the temple. Remember that women and men do not sit
together in a temple. So there's all of this ruckus and people running back and forth and I'm
up on the altar doing my thing while trying to figure out what the fuss is, but of course you
can't stop, you just go on. Well, it turned out that my grandmother was faking a heart attack
in the middle of my bar mitzvah. "Oh my God, I can't breathe!" she cried. "The pain! The
pain!" The ambulance arrived, sirens blaring. I'm trying to outsing the to-do while they

carried her off to the hospital, where of course they found absolutely nothing wrong. But my mother, in retribution, had her admitted to the hospital for observation. And so concluded the sacred portion of my bar mitzvah.

HOW DID YOU RECOVER FROM THAT? IT COULDN'T HAVE BEEN MUCH OF A CELEBRATION.

Don't ask, but we still partied on. If I remember correctly, it was on Eastern Parkway. My mother's friend Shirley was the caterer. My mother is the social queen of the world. She was president of Hadassah for many years. So she and Shirley arranged the whole thing and we had it there on Eastern Parkway in Flatbush. The highlight was that I got to wear a red and black tuxedo. The fabric had sheen to it. It was iridescent. It was hideous. Gaudy as all get-out. Just horrid. I loved it. And then, I fought to make sure that among the other music the band would play, besides all the usual "Alley Cat" and hora stuff, they would play one or two Rolling Stones songs. I was a huge Stones fan. I couldn't get them to play Bob Dylan or Buffy Sainte-Marie, I was already entering my protest-song period, but I did manage to get them to do a couple Rolling Stones songs. And we all danced. And I have eight-millimeter movies to prove it. Silent films were the DVDs of the day.

The highlight of the film is an inordinate amount of footage of Sam Nudleman's wife, Margie, who got SOOO drunk. . . . This was a rather zaftig woman in her seventies or eighties who got up on the dinner table in a green iridescent dress, and danced the hoochie-coochie rubbing herself all over. I mean, you would swear you were watching an age-appropriate stripper for Hugh Hefner's birthday party. Her husband, Sam, kept getting her off the table and she kept getting back up. He just couldn't keep a good woman down.

Meanwhile my poor mother had to go out every hour or so to make sure her mother was still alive, which of course she was, and screaming, "I WANT TO GO TO THE BAR MITZVAH!"

So, all in all, it was a successful affair. But I didn't feel it was the beginning of anything—I really felt it was the end of childhood. It was June. School was over, and I was going to go on to high school. And because I was going to go to a special school in Manhattan, I was leaving most of my friends. I did manage to hang on to one friend, Philomena. Because we were both interested in art we continued on to high school and even college together. So we've been friends from kindergarten right to today. But I knew I was leaving everybody else. My childhood friends were people who, in many cases, still hadn't been to Manhattan. Brooklyn was an insular life for them.

NOW ABOUT THE EXPRESSION "TODAY I'M A MAN." WELL?

I wasn't feeling it. I felt an end. I felt Hebrew school, Saturday morning prayers, the JCH, watching my mother's Friday night mah-jongg games, going for Sunday bagels with my father, listening to my brother's band practice down in the basement—this was no longer my life. I felt removed from the relatives, my friends. I thought it was the end of my life in Brooklyn, even though I went on to live in Park Slope, Brooklyn, for many years. And I definitely felt this was the end of my pretending to believe in the God of my father.

MANY SAY THAT THE CELEBRATION IS SO IMPORTANT AND SO SPECIAL. BUT IN SOME CASES THERE ARE THOSE WHO FIND IT A LITTLE OVER-THE-TOP. WHICH WAY DO YOU LEAN?

People have price priorities, if you know what I mean. My brother is a food and wine connoisseur and will spend money on those things. My mother thinks travel is a worthy place to spend. I prefer shopping for folk art. Still, there is always money, no matter how hard times are, to celebrate family and life's milestones. Can these celebrations get out of hand? Sure. But how many times does a child get bar/bas mitzvahed?

YOU'RE SUCH A CONTROL FREAK. I'M ASSUMING YOU WERE INVOLVED IN THE PLANNING OF YOUR BAR MITZVAH?

Like I said, I was one of those kids—I'm sure the choice of those tuxedos somehow fell on me. And I made sure there were matching matchboxes and table linens and yarmulkes. After all, from that day forth, when the yarmulkes come out for Passover, you know just by the color and fabric whose wedding or bar mitzvah each came from. These are the important things!

DID YOU HAVE ANY TROUBLE LEARNING THE HEBREW PORTION?

I'm dyslexic so I learned it phonetically from a reel-to-reel tape recording. I think I also had it on LP. After four years of Hebrew school, I was okay at writing Hebrew, but I couldn't read it easily.

Me nervous? It didn't bother me. I didn't have the acting bug yet, but I was fine. As the youngest of my peer group all my friends had gone before me. And I attended weekly young people's services in a small temple under the main hall where we kids would read from the Torah every week. It was a smart thing to do. We were used to getting up and reading from the Torah in front of a group. So when it came time to do it at our bar mitzvah, it was not hard. What was hard was watching my grandmother fake a heart attack and then pretending it didn't bother me.

HARVEY WITH HIS FATHER, IRVING, AND BROTHER, RON

Larry King

The suspender-clad King of Talk, Larry King was born Lawrence Harvey Zeiger in Brooklyn, New York, on November 19, 1933, to Russian immigrants Eddie and Jennie Zeiger. Eddie died years before Larry's bar mitzvah, leaving his young son, who dreamed of working in radio, to grow up and work at a variety of jobs, including that of a UPS deliveryman, and most recently as the host of *Larry King Live*. 2007 marks King's fiftieth year in broadcasting. His broadcasting career began in 1957.

Larry King was in his twenties when he got his first radio job in Miami Beach as a DJ for WIOD Radio. In 1960, still in Miami, he found himself in television with his own program on WTVJ-TV, which was a hit with the south Floridians. He went on to host *The Larry King Show* on Mutual Radio Network in 1978, which earned him national recognition. Ted Turner was paying attention and hired him for the brand-new Cable News Network in 1985. *Larry King Live* was a first in television. Viewers could call in their questions and Larry would respond on air. No talk show was rated higher at the time, and by the 1990s, it was CNN's highest-rated program. Celebrities and politicians lined up to appear on the show. It was a place to break news, from Ross Perot's presidential candidacy to the O. J. Simpson murder trial verdict. The Ross Perot–Al Gore NAFTA debate in 1993 broke ratings records in the cable industry when 16.3 million viewers tuned in. International broadcasts of recent exclusive interviews caught the attention of the world: James Frey, Howard Stern, Kobe Bryant, Jennifer Aniston, former presidents Bill Clinton and George H. W. Bush, Bob Woodward and Carl Bernstein on the same day that Deep Throat made himself known, and Elizabeth Taylor. The list is nearly endless.

Larry King is not just talk. He literally became king for a night when he was crowned Bacchus XXXIII in 2001 at Mardi Gras in New Orleans. He's made cameo appearances in movies, among them *Ghostbusters, The Contender,* and *Primary Colors.* And he has been seen on television in shows other than his own, including *The Practice,*

Frasier, and *Arliss.* Larry King is also a man with a heart. After his recovery from quintuple bypass surgery, he started up the Larry King Cardiac Foundation, raising millions to help children and adults with heart problems.

King has five children—Andy, Larry Jr., Chaia, Chance, and Cannon. He is stepfather to Danny Southwick and is married to Shawn Southwick-King.

LARRY KING
THE BOY WHO BECAME KING OF TALK

My bar mitzvah was in 1946 at Temple Tifereth Torah in Bensonhurst, Brooklyn, where I grew up. That was at 22nd Avenue and 83rd Street. We had the ceremony and friends put together a little brunch in the synagogue. After the little sandwiches were finished, I had no major reception, no dancing band. I don't remember invitations. Probably my mother just asked people to come. My father wasn't there, having died when I was nine and a half. My mother, little brother and I had just come off welfare. New York City put us on relief because my mother couldn't go to work and had to take care of me and my brother. New York City bought my first pair of glasses. We had no money. So, it was not a huge bar mitzvah. But all my friends came. I had a lot of friends. It was not the bar mitzvah safari theme. I had the opposite of that. I had a nongigantic bar mitzvah. A strong memory is that I made my speech and I did well because I rehearsed very hard for it.

YOU WERE STUDIOUS AND IT WAS IMPORTANT TO YOU TO DO WELL. WAS IT ENJOYABLE OR A CHORE?

All of the above. I considered myself studious but it was a chore. I wanted to get it just perfect. I wanted everything to be right. I was a perfectionist and I'm even more so now. We did it all in Hebrew. Now they do it in English. That was unheard of then. And then I made a speech. In the speech I remember talking about my father. I had a lot of people crying because I was the little boy without a dad. So, reflecting back, I would say I had that coming of age sooner than thirteen. People were telling me that I was the man of the house, which was a bad thing to do, when I was about ten. They didn't know what they were doing. And they didn't mean any harm. They just said, "You're the man of the house." So I felt there was a lot of responsibility placed on me.

Soon after that, by the way, I lost interest in religion. I would say today that I'm agnostic. But culturally, I'm very Jewish. I like things Jewish. I like the Jewish way of thinking. I like Jewish foods. I like things done well. I'm very Jewish. But I don't know if there's a God or not.

YOU GREW UP TO BE THE KING OF TALK, GIVEN THE GIFT OF GAB. DID YOU POSSESS THOSE QUALITIES AS A TEEN?

Are you out of your mind? I was a nerd! I thought the pimples were due to Hershey bars. I first got interested in girls when I was seventeen. For me, being thirteen was all about the Brooklyn Dodgers.

I think I was popular with the other boys because I was funny. I was a storyteller. They used to call me Zeke the Creek the Mouthpiece. My last name was Zeiger so Zeke came from Zeiger. My nickname was Zeke.

AND WHEN DID YOU GO FROM ZEIGER TO BECOME A KING?

My first day on the air, May 1, 1957.

DO YOU THINK THE BAR MITZVAH CELEBRATION HAS BECOME LESS ABOUT THE CEREMONY AND MORE ABOUT THE PARTY?

Sure, "My bar mitzvah has to be better than yours. . . . Where can I hold my son's bar mitzvah . . . ?" There's a joke about a guy who wanted to throw the best bar mitzvah. He's got all sorts of ideas—paratroopers going into hotels and hiring big-name bands. And finally, someone comes up with the bar mitzvah safari. No one ever did a bar mitzvah safari.

He flies all the people over in 747s. Everybody lines up on elephants. The bar mitzvah boy is up on the first elephant. And the safari doesn't start. So the father goes over to the captain and asks, "Why aren't we starting?" The captain replies, "Well, the Cohen bar mitzvah is ahead of us."

YOU'RE IN A PRIVILEGED SITUATION. AS A FATHER YOURSELF, WHAT TYPE OF CELEBRATION DO YOU SEE DOING ONE DAY FOR YOUR YOUNG SONS?

If it happens, it will be small, because my wife is a devout Mormon, a true believer. They are being raised Mormon, but they understand that they are also Jewish.

I haven't decided if they will be bar mitzvahed. They are six and seven years old. I like the idea of them being bar mitzvahed as a tribute to my mother and father. And Chance, my seven-year-old, calls himself half Jewish and likes being half Jewish. He's in the Beverly Hills public school system and there are a lot of Jews there.

To me the bar mitzvah ceremony is a hundred times more important than the reception after it. The ceremony is an excellent rite of passage as a young man faces manhood. But I don't like the idea of saying to him, "Today you are a Man."

I think it's very important to have some structure in life. To look forward to something like a bar mitzvah. And to learn something from it—that it has some meaning. A party is a party. Anyone can have a party. But the ceremony—I think it has great and lasting meaning. That's what I want to give to my kids. If they have a bar mitzvah, it will not be elaborate.

YOU'RE A WARM AND COMPASSIONATE PERSON. THAT COMES THROUGH ON THE SCREEN. WERE YOU RAISED WITH THOSE VALUES? TO DO THE BEST YOU CAN AND ALSO BE A REALLY NICE GUY?

This is how I was raised. My mother wanted nothing but the best for me. I was spoiled. My mother had only me and my little brother. She never remarried. Anything she could do was for her son Label, which was what she called me. Had I blown up a bank, she would have blamed the bank—maybe they made a mistake in my checking account. She died when I was working in Miami, so she did get to see where my career was heading.

AND BOY, DID IT EVER GO IN THE RIGHT DIRECTION, AND WASN'T IT AT YOUR BAR MITZVAH THAT YOU REALIZED YOU POSSESS THE ABILITY TO NEVER BECOME UNGLUED?

I realized something at my bar mitzvah: I don't get nervous. I've never been terrified of an audience in my life.

DO YOU THINK THAT YOUR BAR MITZVAH MADE YOU THE PERSON YOU BECAME?

My bar mitzvah certainly contributed to who I am today. That speech was the first time I ever spoke in public. I made people cry, which is a kind of power. It's a powerful feeling to have control of an audience. Jackie Gleason told me that he knew he wanted to be on stage when he was six years old. His mother took him to a show. They were in the third row and people were applauding. He turned around to face the people. He didn't want to face the stage. He wanted to face the people. He knew he liked the attention.

I THINK I ALREADY KNOW THE ANSWER TO THIS, BUT DID YOU LIKE BEING IN FRONT OF A CROWD ON THAT PARTICULAR DAY?

Like isn't the word. I loved it. And I still love it. When I go out and make a speech, that's my favorite thing to do, I just do comedy. I tell funny stories. There's no bigger thrill than going on stage at a convention or other gathering, to stand on a stage, have the rapt attention of an audience, and to make them laugh. I always wanted to be a broadcaster. I dreamed of it when I was five years old. I used to look at the radio and imitate the people talking on it. That's all I ever wanted to do. So I'm living out a life's dream.

Jeff Zucker

They call him the Wunderkind, and looking at his résumé, it's no "wunder." At twenty-six years of age, he became the youngest executive producer in *Today* show history. During his eight-year stint, the show climbed into first place and remains NBC's most profitable program. He is credited for the phenomenally successful career of Katie Couric, who became the *Today* show's national correspondent in 1990, with Jeff Zucker as her producer. And *Where in the World* would we be without Matt Lauer? Viewers can thank Jeff Zucker for bringing Matt into millions of homes every morning.

As expected, Zucker's meteoric rise continued. The next stop: president of NBC Entertainment and then in 2007, at just forty-one years old, he was offered the top of the rock, taking helm of NBC Universal, one of the world's leading media companies with revenues of over $16 billion, as president and chief executive officer. In his domain, Zucker is also responsible for a stable of networks including USA, CNBC, MSNBC, Bravo, Sci Fi, and Telemundo. Fans of the hit show *Heroes* consider him a hero for bringing the epic series into their lives. Also under his umbrella, the Universal movie studio and theme parks in Florida and California.

Jeffrey Zucker was born on April 9, 1965, in Miami, Florida. Growing up in Miami, he celebrated his bar mitzvah there. At the time, he was a thirteen-year-old with a full head of hair attending North Miami Junior High School. He graduated from Harvard University in 1986 with a BA in American history. During his four years at Harvard, Zucker was the president of the *Harvard Crimson,* the school's daily newspaper. He added fuel to the rivalry between the paper and the *Harvard Lampoon,* the world's oldest humor magazine, at that time headed by his colleague-to-be, Conan O'Brien.

When he was turned down by Harvard Law School in 1986, Jeff Zucker was hired by NBC to do research to help with the reporting on the 1988 Olympics in Seoul,

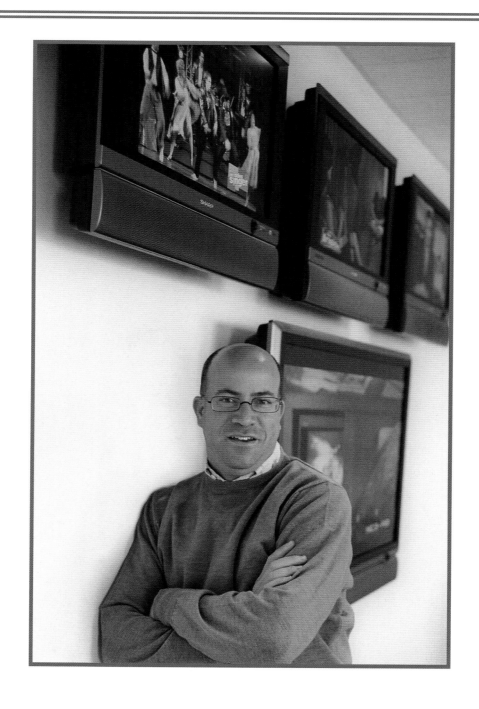

South Korea. He became a producer for the *Today* show a year later and, in January 1992, became the show's executive producer, years before turning thirty. During his tenure, no show could surpass the ratings of the *Today* show, reaching a pinnacle in the 2000–2001 season.

Without Jeff Zucker, Donald Trump might still be just in the building business and Rockefeller Plaza wouldn't be the place where fans flock to see rock concerts. Fans of the *The Apprentice, Las Vegas, Law & Order: Criminal Intent, Scrubs* and *Fear Factor* can applaud Zucker for bringing these shows to the network and the *Today* show's live music to Rockefeller Plaza. As president of NBC Entertainment, a position he took in December 2000, he was in charge of the network's entertainment lineup. Over the next four years, NBC's primetime schedule was a top performer in the major adult eighteen-to-forty-nine demographic age group. In 2004, as president of the NBC Universal Television Group, he enriched the primetime schedule with hits including *My Name Is Earl, The Office, Medium,* the megahit *Deal or No Deal,* and Bravo's *Project Runway.*

Jeff Zucker is married to former *Saturday Night Live* producer Caryn Nathanson. They have four children.

JEFF ZUCKER, ON TOP OF THE ROCK

I have vivid memories of my bar mitzvah. I remember that I wasn't at all intimidated by being in front of people, or scared of it. I enjoyed it. I assumed that's what you did and that it was the normal way you have a bar mitzvah. It was a good experience. You know, my mom planned the whole thing. It probably took a year to do that. I was happy with it, the service and the party. And I remember the party was afterward at the Starlight Roof of the Doral Hotel in Miami Beach. We filled the place. You know that now, of course, most parties are at night, but mine was immediately after the service, and it was really fun. There must have been two hundred people there. I was a big tennis player at the time. So I remember a lot of my tennis friends were there. I had a lot of friends, but no girlfriend.

I remember my bar mitzvah photo. I had that full head of straight hair. Later, it became curly, but it was straight then. My bar mitzvah photo was ridiculous. I was skinny and lanky, with that hair, and I wore a big tie. It was not a bow tie. It was a regular tie and it was big, with a knot.

We were members of the biggest Reform temple in the southeastern United States, which was Temple Israel, in Miami. I went to Sunday school and Hebrew school. I always went to services on the high holy days. I was bar mitzvahed and confirmed at the temple. But we weren't overly religious. We certainly celebrated the Jewish holidays and I had a Jewish education.

DID YOUR BAR MITZVAH HAVE A BIG IMPACT ON YOUR LIFE?

My bar mitzvah was a pretty important day in my childhood. I know I felt proud of what I was doing. I remember the day. I remember the sanctuary. I remember reading from the Torah and that my section was really long because I had been preparing for a long time by going to Hebrew school, and I also had a Hebrew tutor. They kept increasing the amount that I was going to do, but I liked doing the work. I was bar mitzvahed by the senior rabbi at the synagogue, Joseph Narot, who was very well-known. I remember that I was good at the Hebrew. And I can still read Hebrew, even though that was the end of my Hebrew education. I was happy about that. I was glad I did it, but I was happy it was over.

IT'S INTERESTING BECAUSE BACK THEN BAR MITZVAHS SEEMED MORE SUBDUED, OR SHOULD I SAY, LESS COMPETITIVE, THAN THEY ARE TODAY.

It wasn't a competition then. I think it's much more of a competition now. I don't think back then we all looked on it as competition. I mean, the bar mitzvahs of today are out of control and crazy. They're bigger than weddings. And back then, it was a really nice party with a band and dancing. And it wasn't over the top and it wasn't crazy and it wasn't out of control.

AND ANOTHER TALENT SOME MIGHT NOT KNOW YOU POSSESS IS THAT YOU ARE QUITE THE "FANCY DANCER," "THE KING OF THE WHITE MAN'S OVERBITE." WERE YOU BACK THEN? DID YOU ALWAYS HAVE THE MOVES?

Well, clearly. Definitely. For me, it was on display at an early age.

MODEST AS ALWAYS. WHAT WERE YOU LIKE GROWING UP? WHAT TYPE OF KID WERE YOU? A BRAINIAC, I SUSPECT.

I was a good kid who didn't give my parents trouble, who got straight A's in school. I was self-motivated and very competitive. I played tennis my whole life, since I was six years old. I ended up pretty much playing every day of my life. I was a pretty good tennis player. That was my life, school and tennis. Eventually, I went to Harvard, where I still played tennis but only in my freshman year. I stopped after that. And I became the head of the college newspaper. That's why I stopped playing tennis, because I couldn't do both. And I was burnt out on tennis by then. But, you know, my son Andrew is starting to play tennis now, so that's kind of cool.

AND SPEAKING OF YOUR CHILDREN, WHAT WILL YOU DO FOR YOUR DAUGHTER, ELIZABETH, AND THREE SONS, ANDREW, PETER AND WILLIAM WHEN THEY TURN THIRTEEN?

I would like to see all four of my children bar or bat mitzvahed. I would hope to keep the celebrations in perspective. Frankly, I think it's more about the values and the traditions than it is about the religion, not to diminish the religious part of it. But the values and traditions that it instills in a family are really important. It gives you a sense of community and a sense of belonging to a small group and a bigger group. It's a way to bring family together and to bind families, generation to generation. It's a good reminder of where you came from. To me, those are good values.

ARE YOU A RELIGIOUS PERSON, AND, IF SO, HAVE YOU BECOME MORE RELIGIOUS AFTER WHAT YOU HAVE BEEN THROUGH IN THE LAST FEW YEARS, MORE SPIRITUAL I SHOULD SAY?

Yes, because I was sick twice and confronted the possibility of dying. I don't know that it made me more religious, but it made me reconnect with the idea of religion and the traditions and values that I think it brings along.

But I also think having kids puts things in perspective and makes you realize what's important. I don't think you ever lose that competitive spirit, but you figure out how to reprioritize aspects of your life.

Noah Wyle

He's not a doctor, but his bedside manner for ten years on *ER* as Dr. John Carter makes him the numero uno doc in our book. Noah Strausser Speer Wyle was born on June 4, 1971, and raised in Hollywood, California, one of six children born to a Jewish entrepreneur and an Episcopalian orthopedic head nurse who were not avidly religious. The school he attended at the age of thirteen was predominately Jewish, and Wyle's education in Judaism at that time was rather bumpy because he was being educated by other thirteen-year-olds. After he got over the bruises, physical and mental, Wyle went to high school, where he aspired to become a basketball player but, lacking height and ability, decided that acting would be a safer bet.

In high school, he was encouraged by his stepfather, James C. Katz, a film restorer, and acted in several high school plays and attended a theater program at Northwestern University. Wyle opted against college and stayed in Hollywood to study with renowned acting coach Larry Moss. He got his first part at age seventeen in the NBC series *Blind Faith* in 1990. His first feature film role was in the drama *Crooked Hearts* in 1992. He then spent time waiting tables before appearing in *A Few Good Men* in 1992. After that, Wyle returned to the restaurant scene and worked the tables again, and then, after three auditions for *ER,* Wyle started his new career as a doctor, where he stayed for ten years. Although he left *ER* as a regular in 2004, Wyle remains connected to the medical field and works with the nonprofit group Doctors of the World.

He is the artistic producer of the Blank Theater Company in Los Angeles, where young playwrights can showcase their work, and now has the Second Stage Theater in his portfolio, which has produced many successful shows.

Noah Wyle is married to Tracy Warbin and the couple has two children, Owen and Auden. He still plays basketball, only not professionally.

NOAH WYLE
CLOSE, BUT NO CIGAR

I was raised fairly nondenominationally. My father is Jewish and I've been to temple and I've been to my mother's Episcopalian church on Easter and Christmas. That was about the extent of my religious training growing up. I did not have a bar mitzvah, but it was a significant part of my life because all my friends did, and boy, did that have a huge impact on me.

I think, because of that exposure to Judaism as a boy, I now have a certain sense of spirituality. I don't know that I would attribute it to any of the major religions. I think I believe in a higher power. I do believe in grand design. About ten years ago I met a rabbi at a dinner, a fund-raising dinner for Benjamin Netanyahu. And we struck up a conversation at the dinner table. And he was about as unorthodox as an orthodox Jew could be. He broke all my preconceived notions. He was very argumentative. And he was very cynical in some ways and certainly understood my doubts and really enjoyed the debate. And he said, "Well, if you're really curious, why don't you give me a call? And once a week we'll just study together for as long as you want to." I said, "Okay, great!" I spent about three years learning with the rabbi. I was here, he was in Israel. But we'd work on the phone. And he took me in baby steps through the foundations of the religion and the concepts of the higher self and the lower self. At that period in my life, it really made quite a bit of sense to me. I consider those conversations to be the basis of my religious philosophy.

At this point, I haven't spoken to him for a couple of years. But it's one of those comfortable relationships where he's left the door open to me to ask him questions. It's interesting. I got away from it, and it wasn't until I had kids that it came up again in my life. I'm going to have some more questions coming pretty soon. And while I don't think that everything I learned was only about Judaism, I do embrace a lot of aspects of Judaism.

So, unlike a lot of bar mitzvah kids, I learned about my religion as an adult in his twenties. That's a prevailing theme in my life. Most of my expensive education was wasted on me as a youth. I would've appreciated it a lot more now than I did then, that's for sure.

Well, they're very young. My son's three. My daughter's ten months old. So my wife and I—she's not Jewish, by the way—are just starting to have conversations about that. At this point we're leaning toward a philosophy of tolerance and appreciation for all the world's religions and all the best aspects of each of them.

As a little kid, I was pretty skinny. And then those awkward years came around: eleven, twelve, thirteen and fourteen. I went from being long and lean to short and squatty. As far as my clothes sense went, my favorite thing to wear was those elastic-waist pants.

And then, when I was fifteen, I grew six inches in a summer. And I went back to being built like Abe Lincoln again. But for that period of time, at around thirteen, which I refer to as my dark period, I was a pretty chunky little kid.

At that time, I went to a private school in North Hollywood, called Oakwood, that was probably ninety-nine percent Jewish with the exception of me. For about two years straight, every Saturday I was at a bar mitzvah. I remember the first bar mitzvah I ever attended. I was sitting next to my friend Michael Ehrlich, who was a practicing Jew. And we were in the service part of the bar mitzvah. He said to me, "You're not a practicing Jew, are you?" And I said, "No, I'm not." And he said, "Is this your first bar mitzvah?" I said, "It is." And he says, "Okay, well, it's really easy. There's not a lot you need to know. But if you're not a practicing Jew, when they take the Torah out of its cabinet and they bring it around the congregation, all nonpracticing Jews have to close their eyes and hum. And I said, "You'll let me know when that is?" And he said, "Oh, absolutely." So at a certain point in the ceremony, the rabbi goes to the locker and brings out the Torah. My friend gives me a very solemn nod and I closed my eyes and started humming. And I realized, Oh, I must be the only nonpracticing Jew in the whole room. So I heard this little snicker from around me and then I realized I had been had.

It was during that great period of time where break dancing was coming into fashion. And I fancied myself a break-dancer, as chubby as I was. Between the limbo contests, the lip-synching to Bob Seger's songs and break dancing, I definitely had a reputation. I was not a very popular kid. But I vividly remember the time, at Jed Weitzman's bar mitzvah, that I got up and lip-synched to that Bob Seger song "Old Time Rock and Roll," like Tom Cruise did in *Risky Business.* Everybody went nuts. It was one of the first performances in front of my peers I ever gave. And that was a real confidence booster. It actually was a seminal moment. That really was. There were a few of those during my adolescence, although I was a pretty shy kid. But I did have a couple of moments when I shocked myself by doing something that normally would have made me totally panic-stricken. I would get up and do some public speaking or a little skit or sing a song and have it go over really well. And those definitely contributed to my thinking later on that I could do this for a living. That is, as long as my career didn't involve break dancing.

It was at a bar mitzvah where my break-dancing career was cut short. It was because of the worm, a break-dancing move that you really can't fake, unlike some other moves, like spinning on your back. Only one guy in the school could do it well. He was a friend of mine named Mitchell Butler. And I remember it was at Louis Pozen's bar mitzvah party which he had at Chasen's Restaurant. The old Chasen's in Los Angeles. And I was down in the bathroom, in the men's room, and I decided that I was going to break out the worm— and try it that night.

And so I practiced on the bathroom floor. And it went surprisingly well. But then something happened on the actual dance floor. You're supposed to drop down hands first. Then you hit the floor with your chest and then, you know, you kind of roll your way down. Then you flop across the floor. I ended up in a headstand with my legs akimbo over my head. I had no leverage. And it was then, during one of the most panic-stricken moments of my life that I realized that my worm was about to collapse out from underneath me. And it really hurt my back. Then I think I crawled to the side of the stage in shame and hid the anguish I was in.

IS IT TRUE THAT THE WORM DANCE CAUSED YOU TO BREAK YOUR NECK?

Tell me if you can hear something when I move my neck. . . . Okay? That sound was my neck. Whatever I did to my neck on the dance floor at Louis Pozen's bar mitzvah party, I still feel the repercussions of it today.

I don't know what they are like today. But I know that in the late eighties, they were extremely extravagant. Certainly from my view of birthday parties—and my frame of reference was limited to what kind of party a thirteen-year-old could have. But the bar mitzvahs were in these huge restaurants with professional DJs, guys that were icons in Los Angeles. Radio guys like Frazier Smith would come and be the DJ for the party. There was always unbelievable catered food, and while I'm sure that they are more extravagant today, in some ways they were over the top. Even the invitations alone could be very, very impressive.

And then, of course, there were the gifts. You know, when you're thirteen, you're not really thinking about the spiritual aspects of the bar mitzvah. You're looking at the goods. You're thinking that you're thirteen years old and you just got ten grand from your grandmother for memorizing half a page of Hebrew. That sounded damn good to me. Also, I have a lot of fond memories of sucking helium from balloons and sipping Manischewitz out of those little plastic cups. Bar mitzvahs rocked!

Kirk Douglas

With his trademark cleft chin, gravelly voice and rugged good looks, Kirk Douglas is one of our more revered actors, making a name for himself playing, as he once put it, "sons of bitches."

Kirk is also a writer, and he has completed his ninth book, *Let's Face It*, which he dedicated to his grandchildren. *Let's Face It* is a reflection not only of his life, but also of his views on the world today.

Douglas was born Issur Danielovitch in 1916 in Amsterdam, New York. His parents, Belarusian Jews, were poor. He went to St. Lawrence University on a wrestling scholarship and took summer jobs wrestling in carnivals. It was a scholarship to the American Academy of Dramatic Arts that turned his sights to acting. In his debut on Broadway he played a singing Western Union boy in the show *Spring Again*. In 1942, his show business career was interrupted when he enlisted in the U.S. Navy. After his stint in the war, Kirk Douglas returned to acting, and during his vast career he has received three Oscar nominations for his powerful roles in *Champion, The Bad and the Beautiful,* and *Lust for Life* (as Vincent van Gogh). But certainly, two of his most memorable films were *Spartacus* and *Paths of Glory,* in which Douglas powerfully played Colonel Dax, the commander of a French regiment during World War I.

In 1996, Douglas received a special Oscar for "50 years as a moral and creative force in the motion picture community." That was also the year the beloved actor suffered a stroke, partially impairing his speech. But that did not stop him from his work on or off screen, most recently devoting his time to special projects like the restoration of four hundred neglected playgrounds in Los Angeles schools, as well as building playgrounds in Israel for both Arab and Jewish children. Also in Israel, the Douglas Foundation has built a theater close to the Western Wall in Jerusalem, in addition to funding the Anne Douglas Center for Homeless Women on Skid Row in Los Angeles. In 2004, the three-hundred-seat Kirk Douglas Theater in Culver City, California, opened and included among its offerings programs for children and teens.

For his many contributions to this country, Douglas has received many honors. In 1981, he received the highest civilian honor, the Presidential Medal of Freedom, and four years later in France he became First Officer and then a Chevalier of the French Legion of Honor. In 2001, he was awarded the National Medal of the Arts. Douglas also has a star on the legendary Hollywood Walk of Fame, and there is even a street named after him in Palm Springs, California, called—what else?—Kirk Douglas Way.

Douglas, who recently celebrated his 90th birthday, is the father of four sons, actor Michael Douglas and producer Joel Douglas from his first marriage. And in 1954, he married Anne Buydens, his wife of more than fifty-two years. They are parents of producer Peter Vincent Douglas and actor Eric Douglas, who died in 2004. He also has seven grandchildren who call him Pappy.

Never one to say never, Kirk Douglas celebrated his second bar mitzvah on December 9, 1999, at age eighty-three, a day he recalls with great fondness. A hundred ninety-six of his closest friends and family gathered together at the Sinai Temple in Beverly Hills, California, for this momentous occasion.

KIRK DOUGLAS
BARUCH ATAH IS LOVELIER
THE SECOND TIME AROUND

Last week I went to my theater, the Kirk Douglas Theater. They have a workshop production of a musical for teens. The musical was done by kids around thirteen years of age, so that reminded me of my first bar mitzvah in New York. Like all boys at that time, I was more interested in the presents than I was in the bar mitzvah. I don't know if my first bar mitzvah made me a man. But my second bar mitzvah was at eighty-three, well after I became a man. Actually, I like to think that it made me a better man, seventy years after my first bar mitzvah, to have a second bar mitzvah.

If there is an afterlife, and if my mother is in heaven, she will look down and she will smile. That's why I had my second bar mitzvah, for my mother. And, just exactly like I ended my first bar mitzvah, I promised to be a good boy. For me, that's the key. It wasn't about religion. All my study about religion has made me less religious. Because I think the goal of religion is to make you a better person.

DID YOU HAVE TROUBLE LEARNING THE HEBREW AGAIN AT EIGHTY-THREE? WAS IT HARDER THE SECOND TIME AROUND?

I didn't have any trouble learning it. I had enough time to study with the rabbi.

IT MUST HAVE BEEN AN EMOTIONAL AND TOUCHING DAY FOR YOU, YOUR SECOND BAR MITZVAH.

Oh yes, and I was so excited, because so many people were there. All of my sons: Michael and his beautiful wife, Catherine; Joel, Peter, and Eric. Dear friends Larry King, Ernest Borgnine, Red Buttons, Sidney Sheldon, Angie Dickinson, Tony Curtis, Norman Lear, Karl Malden, Monty Hall, Tony Martin, Cyd Charisse, Don Rickles, George Schlatter, Jack Valenti, Barbara Sinatra, Jennifer Jones Simon, Ray Stark, Walter Matthau, Tita Cahn, L.A. mayor Richard Riordan, and Steven Spielberg's mother, Leah Adler, were there. All of the people who were able to be there made me happy. It was a beautiful day.

WERE YOUR SONS BAR MITZVAHED?

No, they were not Jewish because my two wives were not Jewish, and in Judaism the mother must be Jewish for the children to be Jewish. The religion is carried through the mother, not the father. So I decided that they can be whatever they want to be. Because as I said, my philosophy is first to be a good person.

WHY WAS IT SO IMPORTANT FOR YOU TO BE ABLE TO DO THIS AT THIS STAGE IN YOUR LIFE?

I did it to honor my mother.

DID YOU GET UP AND DANCE, DO A LITTLE HORA?

Of course!

AND DID YOUR FRIENDS BRING YOU ENVELOPES OF CASH, OR ANYTHING ELSE?

Not a cent. Some caviar. But no money.

HOW MANY PEOPLE CAN SAY THAT THEY HAD A BAR MITZVAH LATER IN LIFE? YOU COULD BE A TRENDSETTER, KIRK.

I have had people tell me, "Oh, my grandfather wants to have a bar mitzvah because of you." So I have influenced a few people who now plan to have a bar mitzvah. But I don't think it's very common.

WHAT'S THE MAIN DIFFERENCE BETWEEN YOUR TWO BAR MITZVAHS?

At my first bar mitzvah I was pleased with all the presents. As far as the service itself, at the age of thirteen, it didn't have the same significance as my second bar mitzvah had at the age of eighty-three. At thirteen I was too young to appreciate it. At thirteen you say "Today I am a Man." But are you really?

Charles Grodin

For more than three decades, his on-screen roles have made us want to hug him, slap him, but certainly watch him. . . .

And what a diverse career Charles Grodin has had. From dumping the sweet nebbishy wife on their honeymoon for the WASP princess in *The Heartbreak Kid*, to cracking us up as a con conning Robert De Niro in *Midnight Run,* to speaking his mind (for better or worse) as a commentator on *60 Minutes II* and as host of his own CNBC show, which earned him the nickname "the Perpetually Angry Talk Show Host." Well, one thing's for sure—he has done it his way.

Born in Pittsburgh in 1935, he was raised in an Orthodox Jewish household. His maternal grandfather, a Russian Jew, came from a long line of rabbis. Grodin attended the University of Miami but left to study at the Pittsburgh Playhouse and then went on to New York to study with Uta Hagen and eventually Lee Strasberg. He is a member of the Actors Studio. Grodin's big acting break came in 1968 when he played the obstetrician we all love to hate in the horror film *Rosemary's Baby.* Grodin jokes how to this day people are still "furious" with him that he did not help Mia Farrow's character, and tell him so openly on the street.

In the nineties, his career "went to the dogs," literally, with films *Beethoven* and *Beethoven's 2nd*, which were his two biggest-grossing movies. He left the movies at the peak of his career to be a stay-at-home dad when his son entered first grade. He began his talk show on CNBC after that. It was nominated as best talk show on cable every year there were awards.

He returned to the movies in 2007. Currently, he is a commentator for CBS News, where he is heard all across the country. He is also working on a book that will be published in the fall of 2007. His play, *We 3,* opens at the Long Wharf Theatre in New Haven in 2007. I caught up with him at a very quaint West Side theater where he was rehearsing one of his plays and we talked about the day the boy "became a Man."

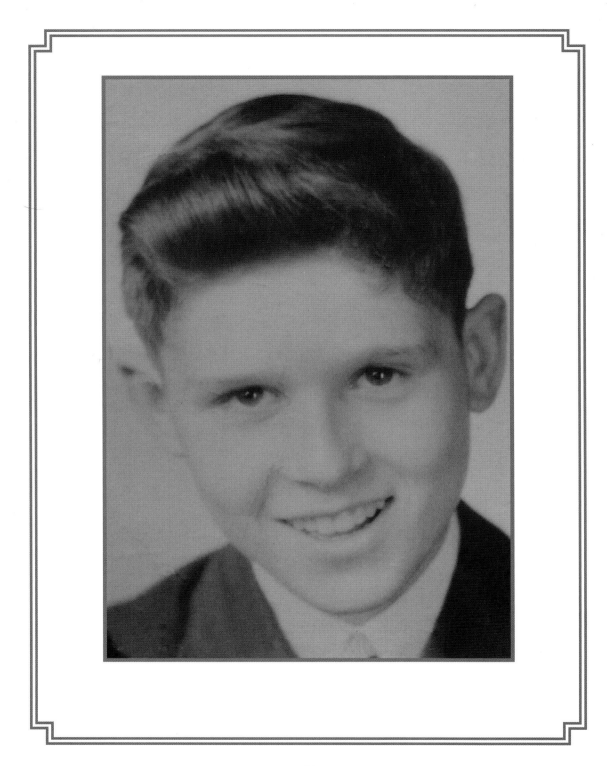

CHARLES GRODIN
ANYTHING BUT A HEARTBREAK KID

I was raised in an Orthodox Jewish home, but I wouldn't call myself a dedicated Jew today. What I would call myself is someone who is dedicated to the principles that every religion would espouse. And I really do trace that back to my religious upbringing, although it doesn't manifest itself in Jewish rituals or anything else. However, if I sense any anti-Semitism, I become more Jewish.

I was thrown out of Hebrew school when I was eleven because I asked the rabbi what the Hebrew words meant on the blackboard too many times for his comfort level, and he resented it. (This wasn't the first time I got into trouble at school—a year earlier I was impeached as president of my fifth-grade class. That was just for talking incessantly, which I still do, but now I get paid to do it.)

YOU CHALLENGED THE RABBI?

Well, sort of. I just said, "What do the words mean that we're reading?" It seemed to be a good question to me. And he thought it was rude or something. I said, "Why can't we know what we're saying?"

It seemed like a logical thing. And he actually kicked me out of the Hebrew school, which was good because I then went to a smaller place where the father of my closest friend at that time, a man named Rabbi Morris Kaplan, took me under his wing. And then I went and studied some with my grandfather, who was a Talmudic scholar in Chicago. I was part of a triple bar mitzvah in Chicago, even though I'm from Pittsburgh. I was bar mitzvahed with my cousin and somebody else.

A THREE-FOR-ONE DEAL? DID YOU GET A BETTER PRICE?

Yeah, it was a three for one. I wasn't involved in costs at that time. The rabbi wrote my speech. It got applause in an Orthodox synagogue, which I don't believe is allowed. The applause was not for my delivery, but it was 1948, the year the state of Israel was founded, and the rabbi had crafted a brilliant speech around the founding of Israel. I think the applause may be what encouraged me to think about show business, although it quickly left my head pretty much after the bar mitzvah. Also, after my bar mitzvah I stopped doing every religious ritual except being guided by the principles of how to be a good person, which guide me today.

SPEAKING OF SHOW BUSINESS, YOU WERE AWARE OF IT AT YOUR BAR MITZVAH, BUT WHAT FIRST TURNED YOU ON TO PERFORMING?

This happened at the Hebrew school I went to before I was kicked out. I was wandering around in the basement, and I opened up a door. And there was a girl singing . . . I think it was "The Man I Love." "Someday he'll come along/The man I love." I was just transfixed. It felt magical; a person is standing on a stage performing. It was a magic moment, the first time I saw somebody perform live. I was eight years old . . . and I remember standing there and just staring, thinking I had never seen anything like that before.

YOU WERE RAISED IN AN ORTHODOX HOME. WHAT ABOUT YOUR OWN FAMILY. WAS YOUR SON BAR MITZVAHED?

No, he wasn't. My wife signed him up for something, but he never went. He doesn't really believe in any kind of ritualistic religion. He's nineteen. My daughter, who's older, also doesn't formally practice any religion, but both consider themselves Jewish. They both have reputations as being very nice people. This is what I'm most proud of.

CONSIDERING YOU WERE ALWAYS AN INCESSANT TALKER, I BET YOU WELCOMED THE MOMENT TO ADDRESS THE CROWD—NOT NERVOUS AT ALL, RIGHT?

I don't remember being nervous. I remember my grandfather just saying to me that he liked what I was doing. I was just trying to do it as best I could. Sometime either just after that or before that, I played the lead in the grammar school graduation play. And I remember that I learned my lines and everybody else's, too, and I'd whisper the lines to them when they forgot them. So it's just this kind of diligence thing.

But I don't remember being nervous. I'm usually so focused on the job at hand that it's one of the things that has really served me. This is not to say that I don't know the difference between a Broadway opening night and sitting at home on my sofa. But I'm so focused on the job at hand that I don't really get as nervous as you might think people would get.

If you just concentrate on what you're supposed to, and don't worry about what anybody else thinks, that's the best thing you can do.

Donny Deutsch

Advertising guru and TV host Donny Deutsch doesn't shrink away from the limelight. His first major appearance was on November 22, 1957, the day he was born in Queens, New York. His second was at his bar mitzvah, also in Queens, on November 14, 1970. Most recently, he can be seen on his own successful show *The Big Idea with Donny Deutsch* on CNBC, and as guest host from time to time on *Squawk Box* and *Kudlow & Cramer*. Because he is not short on energy, Deutsch also has independent film projects in the works and collaborated on a book with Peter Knobler, *Often Wrong, Never in Doubt*, published in 2005.

Donny Deutsch grew up in New York City and went to Van Buren High School in Queens Village. He graduated from the Wharton School of the University of Pennsylvania and then started his career at advertising giant Ogilvy & Mather, about which Deutsch says, "They should have fired me." In 1983, he went to work in his father's advertising agency. In 1984, he was running the agency and had changed its name to Deutsch, Inc. Attracting big accounts with his very creative team, the agency developed and launched award-winning campaigns. Among his clients: Pfizer, Tanqueray, Coors, Bank of America, Mitsubishi, and IKEA, for which he designed a groundbreaking campaign featuring a gay couple. Besides being proud of his bar mitzvah, Deutsch is also proud to have worked on the 1992 Bill Clinton for President campaign.

DONNY DEUTSCH
THE BOY WITH "THE BIG IDEA"

I don't think anybody ever remembers their tenth birthday, but the bar mitzvah is a milestone in your childhood. I remember all the planning that went into it and how it brought my family together. I had one grandfather and one grandmother there, and they've since passed on. I can remember what they were wearing. My grandfather cut the challah. His name was Leo, and he actually got drunk. He'd recently lost his wife, my grandmother, maybe a year earlier. He got pretty lit up that day, I remember. He was having a good time. And I remember the look on my dad's face; he just couldn't be prouder, you know, just watching me read the Torah. It was nice.

I remember being nervous about reading my portion of the Torah, even though I knew that everybody gets through it. I remember my bar mitzvah as a wonderful party. My mother jokes to this day that when we came walking in, they played music, and they played "Mister Wonderful," or something like that, and I got a big smile on my face.

DONNY AND HIS GRANDFATHER

I just remember being with all my friends. It was a long time ago, over thirty years ago, but it stays with you. You live with the pictures over the years. And what staggers me now is when I see my parents in the photos, and my dad was forty-one, six years younger than I am now. And I still have a lot of my childhood friends. It was just a wonderful, wonderful time.

CONSIDERING YOU HAD SO MANY FRIENDS, DID YOU HAVE A LARGE PARTY?

It was probably two hundred people, which was a decent size. Today there are these huge extravaganzas. Bar mitzvahs then didn't have *Star Wars* themes, and entertainers showing up, or whatnot. It was a celebration on a Saturday afternoon. Just the typical band, and in those days you did the bunny hop, and it was fun. It was just a good time.

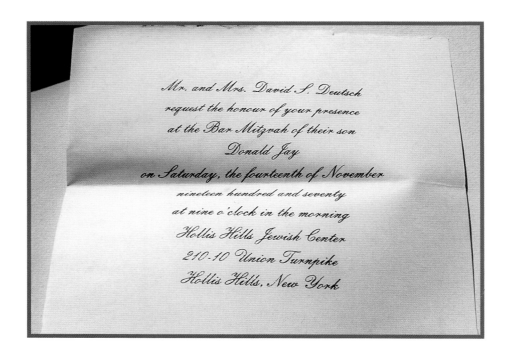

DONNY AND HIS SISTER, AMY, WITH THEIR PARENTS, FRANCINE AND DAVID

DID YOU FEEL THE TRANSITION FROM BOY TO MAN AT THAT MOMENT?

No! I go to a lot of bar and bat mitzvahs now, of my friends' kids. Most of the girls at that age have gone through puberty already, and they look five years older than the boys. Most of the boys are still boys, and I was also. Technically, I was, in the Jewish religion, going through the rites of manhood. But I don't think I had gone through the physical changes so I was still a real little kid, with the true cherub face.

CLEARLY, YOU'RE VERY OUTGOING AND ENGAGING. WERE YOU LIKE THAT AT THIRTEEN?

I always had a lot of friends. That came easy to me. I was very popular. And I remember, I can see looking at the pictures now, my closer friends were the ones next to me on the dais. Now that seems very funny. My best friend since first grade, Perry Schorr, was there. My other closest friend was not there, Cindy Mangano. Now she's an attorney. I must have been in a fight with her, because she wasn't at my bar mitzvah, and to this day we still bust balls about that. Nadine Whiteman was my girlfriend. She was my first love in sixth grade, and we were still together in eighth grade, when I had my bar mitzvah. It was November 14, 1970, and Nadine was my girlfriend. She's somewhere in North Carolina now.

HOW DID YOU FEEL ABOUT BEING THE CENTER OF ATTENTION? LOVED IT, I BET?

My mother will, to this day, talk about how happy I was. I clearly don't mind being the center of attention, you know, and I like the spotlight, that's kind of fun. And look, that's your first day as a young man. I was excited. I just remember being so excited; the buildup to it . . . I remember having just a really good time.

HOW WAS IT STUDYING THE TORAH?

Difficult. They had a guy, a sexton, at my temple named Frank Strauss. He's probably since passed on. And his main thing was getting all the bar mitzvah guys prepared. We would

DONNY AND FRIENDS

73

take the lessons with him, and we got through it. I remember the first sentence of my Torah portion. It's something that just sticks in your head. But I can't really read Hebrew that well today. I went to Hebrew school for five years, but it didn't stick, unfortunately.

ARE YOU A RELIGIOUS PERSON NOW?

No, not really. I mean, I go to synagogue on the high holy days. Actually, I still go to the place where I was bar mitzvahed, which is the Hollis Hills Jewish Center in Queens. I go back there for the high holy days. What's happening there now is what's happening in a lot of Jewish neighborhoods in the city—the neighborhood is changing. It used to be half Jewish and half Irish. Now it's a tremendous melting pot, and you don't have enough of a generation of Jews coming in. The temple is getting very old. So, I helped them out, and paid off their mortgage, and now it's the Deutsch Hebrew School. So I go back, and I always celebrate the high holy days there. I have a tremendous affection for it and connection to it.

IS IT REFORM, CONSERVATIVE?

Conservative. When you go to some of these Reform ones, they're doing folk songs. I like the more traditional. The cantor from the shul where I grew up, who was the cantor then at my bar mitzvah, officiated at my last wedding. So, you know, I like to stay close to my roots.

Richard Dreyfuss

In *The Goodbye Girl,* Richard Dreyfuss played an out-of-work actor (and won an Oscar for his efforts), but unlike his character in the movie, the leading man has worked steadily as an actor for more than forty years in some forty films, starting with an un-credited part in *The Graduate* in 1967. *American Graffiti* in 1973 earned him well-deserved praise and a paycheck of $480 per week. His memorable performances in the Steven Spielberg films *Jaws* and *Close Encounters of the Third Kind* still keep movie watchers on the edge of their seats today. In *What About Bob?* he plays a psychiatrist who runs out of patience with a patient who is driving him crazy. In the 1995 film *Mr. Holland's Opus,* he returned to the screen on a more serious note as a dedicated music teacher struggling with family issues. In 2006, he was one of two lucky people to survive in *Poseidon.* Richard Dreyfuss has the distinction of being the only actor who starred in films directed by both George Lucas and Steven Spielberg that were not part of the *Star Wars* or *Indiana Jones* series.

Richard Dreyfuss began acting at the West Side Jewish Community Center and at the age of nine, played Zionism founder Theodore Herzl. At fifteen, just before his confirmation, he got a role in the center's production of *In Mama's House.* He attended San Fernando Valley State College for a year and then got parts in several television shows, including *Bewitched, The Big Valley,* and *Peyton Place.* Then along came *The Graduate. . . .*

His work as a political activist is noteworthy, including his efforts to bring peace to the Middle East. He's determined to bring civics back into our classrooms. His feelings on politics mirror his philosophy on religion: don't take any information for granted. Ask questions and do some investigating until you find an answer that satisfies you.

RICHARD DREYFUSS AND HIS SON BEN

CONFIRMATION CLASS PHOTOGRAPH

During the Vietnam War, Richard Dreyfuss was a conscientious objector, but these days he participates in Civil War reenactments in his spare time.

Richard Dreyfuss married Svetlana Erokhin in 1996 and has three children from a former marriage.

THE APPRENTICESHIP OF RICHARD DREYFUSS

When I was eight, my family moved from New York to L.A. In New York we had lived in a progressive Jewish neighborhood. Everyone was Jewish. There were no Christians; it was a "Jewish progressive red diaper baby" area. When I would ask my father, "Why don't we practice Judaism?" He would answer, "I don't have to practice. I'm very good at it."

He told my brother and me that he had been visited by elders from the synagogue. They said that Dad owed us an introduction to Judaism. Then our dad told us, "I may not practice Judaism. But I want you to understand it and so I'll give you a choice. I'll allow you to choose between a bar mitzvah and confirmation. You may have one or the other, whichever you prefer. It doesn't matter to me which way you go. I'll describe what both are like, bar mitzvah and confirmation, to help you make a choice." In confirmation there are questions and answers and epics and you discuss what's right and what's wrong." And I said, "I'll be confirmed." It was clear that he had no patience for the other one. I was nine or ten years old.

I didn't realize it at the time, but my Jewish education could have ended at thirteen. But since my father didn't point that out, I stayed in Jewish education classes for years and was confirmed at sixteen. Luckily, by that time, I was in love with confirmation class. There was a lot of discussion of what is right and wrong and what is good and evil and why is Judaism important and who are the Jews and who are they not. Every week, the class was loaded with debates on Judaism and history. It was more than memorizing Hebrew. We could discuss incredible issues, and my rabbi, Isaiah Zeldin, would say something to the class like "Moses was the epitome of truth." And my hand would shoot up and I would say, "Why?" Nothing gave me more joy that saying to the rabbi, "I disagree with you."

He would talk to me about what these stories meant. I would tell him what I thought these stories meant and I was always arguing with him. And so at confirmation, Rabbi Zeldin made a speech saying there's "one in every class" and that I was a dissenter from the way he had presented the ethics of Judaism but not a dissenter from the ethics. I would say that I took pride in asking questions, and I learned during the course of that time to fall in love with being Jewish.

I was faced with what is great and wonderful about being Jewish. I believed that we were the chosen people and we were chosen to illuminate mankind. I had never for a moment had any self-loathing or self-hatred or anything like what people talk about. I only had a kind of pride and affection for my history. So when I was about eleven or twelve, I remember saying to my mother one day, "I'm the luckiest kid in the world." And she said, "Why?" And I said, "I'm white, Jewish and American."

And she, being a socialist, communist, and progressive Jew, decided to take my education in hand a bit. I was introduced to politics, and the only thing that happened to me during the next forty years was that I became more proud of being American and more proud of being Jewish and that being white is a nonissue to me."

YOU WERE SO EVOLVED AS A TEENAGER. I WOULD IMAGINE THAT THE MAJORITY OF YOUR FRIENDS HAD TO HAVE BEEN BAR MITZVAHED. DID YOU START TO WONDER, WHY DIDN'T I DO WHAT THEY DID?

No, I felt like I had been given a free pass. I went to all my friends' bar mitzvahs and I ate a lot of cake and watched one friend start to pee in his pants in front of the congregation, which was really horrifying.

Aside from that incident, I guess the kids getting bar mitzvahs enjoyed it and were proud of it. But I was interested in something else and, for me, it had no appeal. I would have had trouble with every moment of the experience, starting with learning the language. I would have hated it because I would not have been learning the answers to my questions. Who are we and who are we meant to be and what is our ambition? Getting the answers didn't seem to be part of the bar mitzvah experience.

I did go to a whole bunch of bar mitzvahs and I thought they were all as boring as going to temple, and as far as prayer goes, I was never a person of ritual. I was never a person of prayer. I was always kind of irritated by God. I hated going to temple and participating in the ritual. But I loved listening to the rabbi pontificate because I loved the idea of, you know, getting up and telling people how to live. Apparently, I had a rabbi lurking in me and I didn't know it until I started to get into Jewish politics and Israeli politics and I started to write speeches, and I found myself possessed by the spirit of a Reform rabbi from New Jersey.

No, I never felt that I would be a man because I memorized a passage of Hebrew text, and I never thought that I would need to get a really great silver candle or a TV from my uncle to make me a man. It never occurred to me that the gifts were of any importance whatsoever. I came from a middle-class family. I had no desires that couldn't be acquired. So it was never put to the test. What I wanted in those days were books, and I got books.

DID YOU HAVE A CELEBRATION AT YOUR CONFIRMATION?

We had a graduation ceremony and that's when the rabbi made a speech that included mention of me, because I was the "rebel in the community." Other than that, no. Given what I think about rituals, it would have been silly. I realize now as we're talking that I didn't get confirmation gifts. I mean pens or ties or anything. There was nothing.

CONSIDERING YOU WERE THE "REBEL IN THE COMMUNITY," DID YOU HAVE A LOT OF FRIENDS OR WERE KIDS INTIMIDATED BY YOU?

I was popular. But more than that, I was vivid. A lot of people liked me, a lot of people didn't. When you move into a new school and you're short and all the guys are bigger, you have to immediately develop a skill that will keep them off you. My skill was my mouth. They always knew that there was no reward for beating me up because I was going make them feel like shit anyway. I would say to them, "So what—you're going to hit me? You'll still be wrong."

My kids were the product of a mixed marriage—she was Protestant and I was Jewish. We're divorced now and so they never really got the dose of Jewishness that I had. Now that they're mostly grown—my daughter's twenty-two, my son is twenty, my youngest son is sixteen—they are curious about it. I wasn't there, so I couldn't help them.

And that was a tragedy for me. I, who had never thought of ritual and tradition and going to temple (and I still don't), was bereft. I felt terrible that I couldn't give them what I call the Jewish home.

I started when I was eight or nine and I graduated when I was sixteen. So where I came out was that to me Judaism was some six hundred laws about how to live on the planet Earth together, and how to live in a community and how to be separate and isolated as the Jews have been, especially in the fifties and sixties, when there was proof that people wanted to kill every Jew on earth, and why was that? I was so proud of being Jewish. My confirmation led me into pondering the process of thought and being Jewish. Being Jewish meant thinking. Judaism has a great meaning to me. It's about right and wrong and that you don't treat Jews better than other people, in fact, we are other people. That we represent all of mankind, the best and worst of men, so we can only learn from the Jews by the Jews being virtuous. I've always hated rituals because it absolves people of the responsibility of being good. Does the bar mitzvah really give us an understanding of who we are and who we are in the world as Jews? I don't think so. Really, Judaism is about behavior. It isn't about heaven and hell. It's about your behavior as a good person, and that's the great opportunity of Judaism.

AS AN ACTOR, ESPECIALLY AN OSCAR WINNER, YOU HAVE ALL THESE OPPORTUNITIES TO PLAY DIFFERENT ROLES. DO YOU THINK THAT YOUR FEELINGS ABOUT JUDAISM CONTRIBUTED TO WHO YOU ARE AS AN ACTOR?

You know that in Canada *The Apprenticeship of Duddy Kravitz,* the book and the film, are iconic. It's one of the most important books ever written. It was the first time that anyone had ever taken a character like Duddy and held him up to the world. He was a guy who became a pusher, all of the clichés the gentiles called the Jews. The Jewish communities were saying, "Oh, but we shouldn't wash our dirty linen in public." And I thought, Now there's a great controversy and people will go to see the movie and it'll be a big hit.

But it was a small controversy and people didn't go to the movie and it wasn't a big hit, although it has a cultural space. I wanted people to go to see the movie.

DID YOUR PARENTS SUPPORT YOUR DOING THAT FILM?

They supported me in whatever I wanted to do. Don't you think that's very Jewish? My parents said, "You know, life is about passion."

Howie Mandel

Turning fifty was fabulous for Howie Mandel; he really made the right deal when he agreed to host the megahit game show *Deal or No Deal* on NBC. Millions now know him as the man who can help them make a million, or not. After more than thirty years in show business, funnyman Howie Mandel is now laughing all the way to the bank.

Born on November 29, 1955, Howie Mandel grew up in Toronto, Ontario, and attended Beth David B'nai Israel Beth Am's Hebrew school. As a young man, he had a carpet business before making the career move that would change his life. One night in 1979, while on vacation, Mandel attended an amateur event at L.A.'s Comedy Store club. Unable to resist his prescient friends' daring him to try out, Mandel did, and impressed a producer, who got him a spot on the game show *Make Me Laugh.* Howie Mandel made them laugh and went on to work in a wide variety of entertainment venues: network and cable television, movies and theater. In 1982, he became a doctor, on TV. For the next six years, he was Dr. Wayne Fiscus on the Emmy Award–winning *St. Elsewhere.* Then, in 1990, he became creator, executive producer and voice of the cartoon children's series *Bobby's World.* Also an Emmy Award–winner, the show was on Fox for eight seasons and is now in syndication, appearing six days a week in sixty-five countries. Mandel says that the show's continuing success is because the stories are believable, because they're inspired by real life. He had already proved his appeal to children as the voice of the character Gizmo in the 1984 film *Gremlins.*

Howie Mandel continues to be seen in comedy specials on television and on *The Tonight Show with Jay Leno,* showing the hidden camera segments that he's known for. In 1998 and 1999, he hosted *The Howie Mandel Show* talk show and is who Regis Philbin first

thinks of when it's time to go on vacation. Mandel frequently steps in as a guest host on *Live with Regis and Kelly.* Live performances are a big part of the Mandel's long career as a performer, and every year he does some two hundred concerts in the U.S. and Canada.

Residing in Los Angeles, Howie Mandel and his wife, Terry, have three children.

HOWIE MANDEL, THE REAL DEAL, EVEN AT THIRTEEN

I was bar mitzvahed on December 7, 1968. The reason I know that it was December 7 is because there was a lot of talk about Pearl Harbor. I was Canadian; Pearl Harbor doesn't have the same significance, but every day we talked about how it's a special day. And the fact that all the women there were named Pearl. All my mother's friends, ironically, seemed to be named Pearl, but for old Jewish women, that's like being named Smith.

There were all these speeches about Pearl Harbor. It's just a big mess in my mind. It was just this huge responsibility, and the only light at the end of the tunnel was that I didn't have to go to the Hebrew school anymore. I was told I could go up until my bar mitzvah. It was like a really bad graduation ceremony as far as I was concerned.

You know, these celebrations never really made sense to me as a Jew. The word *celebrate,* as we learned it, has a sense of festivity and fun and laughter and holiday. But it never really felt that way. When I got off of school for Yom Kippur, which was supposed to be a holiday, and the Yom Kippur celebration, there was no food or water. That doesn't lend itself to celebrating. The earliest memory I have of a celebration was inviting a lot of people over to the house for a bris, which was a celebration. I didn't really understand the celebration connected with the slicing off of the end of one's penis. And they serve and cater. I never really understood that.

Well, I just remember a lot of strangers. I was very short. They said today I'm a man but I
didn't have a job. I didn't earn a living. I lived with other people. I shared a room. So how
does this make me a man, I ask you? I was at a big party with music. I didn't know how to
do the alley cat. A lot of people were doing the alley cat. I saw a lot of asses. And a lot of
gowns with sequins.

I was four foot ten. Two years later, at fifteen, I was on the wrestling team, and I was in
the eighty-nine-pound class. So I know I weighed less and was shorter at my bar mitzvah.

I was not popular. First of all, in my school, I was one of very few Jews. And when
you're four foot ten and you weigh seventy-something and you explain to all your non-
Jewish friends that you can't go out this Saturday because you're having a party celebrating
the fact that you're a man. And this is a guy who had a woman's voice. My voice hadn't
changed. And I had to shave. I stood on a crate to see up to the altar to read from the
Torah.

WHAT ABOUT GIRLS? WERE YOU A BABE MAGNET BACK THEN?

I was just very different. I was very little, very tiny. I couldn't meet girls, but I figured out
that I could get close to them because I looked like a girl. I could stand in the girls' bathroom in front of the mirror brushing my hair, and nobody would know that I was a boy.

WERE YOU FUNNY? DID YOU HAVE A SENSE OF HUMOR?

I think I looked funnier than I actually was.

THERE WAS NO BUDDING COMEDIAN AT THAT POINT IN YOUR LIFE?

The budding comedian really didn't come out until I was twenty-three. I was not funny at
thirteen. Not at that point in my life. And at my bar mitzvah, nobody I knew was there. In
fact, I wonder if this has happened at any other bar mitzvah. I remember wandering around
aimlessly, but as a Jew, that's what we do. We wander. I was wandering around this room,
and older people who I had never seen in my life and have never seen since would come up
to me and go, "You don't know who I am, do you? Guess who I am? You don't remember

me, do you? I was at your bris." I don't remember anybody from my bris. But they hand you envelopes and I was stuffed with envelopes. And I didn't get to keep any of it.

WHAT DO YOU MEAN? WHAT HAPPENED? IT WENT TOWARD COLLEGE?

No, toward the bar mitzvah. It went toward the bar mitzvah.

THEY TOOK YOUR ENVELOPES TO PAY FOR THE PARTY?

Yes. And let me tell you the best part of the night, or the worst. My father's best friend was a courtroom sketch artist. So they hired this sketch artist from the court to capture the bar mitzvah.

YOU MEAN TO TELL ME THEY HIRED A SKETCH ARTIST INSTEAD OF A PHOTOGRAPHER?

Yes, can you believe it? So we had, like you see on the news, courtroom sketches of my bar mitzvah. This is what we did and it made the evening miserable: it would take him ten minutes to sketch us in a certain pose . . . "Oh, you're dancing with your mother. Just stay right there." We weren't allowed to move as he sketched us. We had no video, just these pencil sketches of the evening, and in all of them I'm standing uncomfortably still in bad positions.

Oy, what a night!

Andy and Josh Bernstein

Born and raised in New York City, twins Josh and Andy Bernstein have made careers out of helping others to cope with the challenges of their surroundings. Yet while Josh's clients master the skills needed to survive in the wilderness, Andy teaches his audiences the skills needed to manage the stress of the corporate jungle. Despite their different environments, both have earned widespread acclaim with their constructive and entertaining approaches to common—and uncommon—problems.

Andy Bernstein is the founder of ActivInsight, an intelligent new way to eliminate stress and handle change. A Phi Beta Kappa graduate of Johns Hopkins University, Andy spent many years studying a wide variety of transformational processes. His work has been featured in *O* magazine, and he now teaches ActivInsight at companies like Johnson & Johnson, Lehman Brothers, and Merrill Lynch; at nonprofits like Phoenix House; and through top business schools like Wharton.

While Andy explored the inner world of the mind, Josh headed into the wild. Josh is the president and CEO of the Boulder Outdoor Survival School, the oldest and largest wilderness survival school in the world. In 2004, Josh became host of the History Channel's hit show, *Digging for the Truth*, sharing his enthusiasm for travel and adventure to active and armchair explorers alike. In 2007, Josh changed channels, moving to the Discovery Channel where he is hosting and producing series and specials on a variety of subjects, such as the environment, archaeology, and anthropology. With a winning combination of talent and rugged good looks, Josh has been featured in publications such as *Men's Vogue* and the Style section of *The New York Times*.

Josh (left) and Andy Bernstein in Central Park

Josh (left) and Andy Bernstein reading their haftarah

JOSH AND ANDY BERNSTEIN
THE JOSH AND ANDY SHOW

JOSH: I think that the bar mitzvah is one of the few remaining rites of passage in our world today. It's an event that celebrates the transition from boy to man. So for me, it was a big event. It was the thing that I, and we, worked so hard for. And it was nice that my brother and I were working so hard together. Twice the fun, half the work and twice the party.

We split the haftarah portion. I did the first portion. Andy did the second half. It was twenty-six years ago so it's hard to remember the specifics. But I recall investing a lot of time in it, and wanted to not screw up.

We had our bar mitzvahs on February 4, 1984, at Park Avenue Synagogue on East 87th Street at Madison Avenue in New York. It was three weeks before our thirteenth birthday. We both invited our friends and there must have been about a hundred forty or a hundred fifty people there.

WHAT ADVICE WOULD YOU GIVE THIRTEEN YEAR OLDS WHO ARE GOING TO BE READING THIS BOOK?

JOSH: You should smile, do your best, it will all be over soon. But at the same time, you're surrounded by the people who love you the most in a setting where the most learned of rabbis and scholars are right there next to you to help you. So smile, and say your haftarah.

ANDY: And then dance.

JOSH: And then dance. I do remember that we had the best party. Being the Bernstein twins, we could have twice the party at once. The guest list was twice as long. So we had the best bar mitzvah in our class.

ANDY: It was great. It was at the Pierre [hotel]. There was a fifteen-person band with smoke machines and T-shirts for the kids. And we had these beautiful cakes that I think we may still have pieces of in the freezer. And we danced and we had so much fun. Our friends were there, almost our whole class from Horace Mann, which is a private school in Riverdale. There were maybe a hundred people in our grade and most of them were Jewish.

I do remember that the girls were taller than we were.

JOSH: It was a coming together of the families, our mom's side and her friends, and our dad's side and his friends, and our friends. We merged them together and we had a big party. Our mom's grandmother was old-school, old-world Judaism, Orthodox, a kosher home. And so, Judaism and the importance of Jewish culture, the tradition, the family values were very clear in that household. And our father, who grew up in Israel—Judaism was just a fact of life. It was more the secular version of Judaism. You were born in Israel, you were Jewish, and so the idea of the bar mitzvah ceremony wasn't as strong in his family. Being raised in our mom's house after the divorce instilled in us the importance of Jewish tradition. It meant a lot more to her. Our dad was very proud of our bar mitzvah after the fact.

ANDY: There was a lot of tension in our family between our mother and father after the divorce. It was not a friendly divorce. And our father would have some difficulty in public appearances with our mother.

He came to the bar mitzvah, and not only was he in the photos and cutting the cake with our mother and us, and doing all of the things that one does, but he was there emotionally as well. And he took our mother aside and said, "You've done a great job raising our boys."

JOSH: Which was a huge thing for a not-very-forthcoming Israeli man to say.

ANDY: I think that the spirit of it being a rite of passage and a point of transformation is that way for everyone. It's a chance to really step out and reflect.

WERE EITHER OF YOU NERVOUS?

JOSH: I don't remember being nervous. But I remember having to sing in front of all these people in a squeaky voice because your voice is changing. And it was like, God, I hope I don't mess up.

ANDY: I remember being nervous. And one boy in our class—he's a legend now—threw up. Or he partially threw up during his bar mitzvah. When he got up there, there was a gagging thing happening. Everyone was discussing it, because we were all having our bar mitzvahs around the same time period. And so I remember feeling really nervous and thinking, "Oh my God, I hope I don't live on as the one who . . ." And Josh went first, and then I went.

And we had partnered symbolically with two Russian Jews. So he represented a Russian Jew, I represented a Russian Jew, and they bar mitzvahed through us. It was really a beautiful symbol of that rite of passage that Josh was talking about.

JOSH: We each had the name of a boy in Russia. Edward Doks was one of them. What I understood from my thirteen-year-old perspective was that they lived in a community where Judaism was not openly encouraged, and there was no way for them to have a bar mitzvah. So through this twinning, it's like we were basically bar mitzvahing them through our ceremony. I asked my teacher if she could help me write a letter to my twin in Russia. And then I got his mom on the phone and we read the letter to her: "Hi, my name is Josh Bernstein, and I'm twinning your son in a bar mitzvah this weekend." And she started crying, saying "Thank you, thank you." It was very special. I think that . . . that that was a way for . . . for me to connect with the culture of Judaism around the world and the significance of that tradition.

Later on, my perspective on Judaism changed. I spent a year after college studying Judaism, the mysticism and halacha in Jerusalem. I'd say I know far more now than I did at the age of thirteen, or even just growing up in America. Judaism in the Diaspora is very different than Judaism in Israel. And then that is very different from traditional Judaic culture. The one thing that impressed me the most in Israel was how deep the tradition is, how rich the culture is, and how family oriented it is. There's so much to the laws about how you treat your spouse, how you raise your children, what kind of household you create, and the significance of the heritage gets passed on from one generation to the next. And so, I came away from that year in Israel, 1993–1994, feeling like this is so much more than just saying a few words in temple on your bar mitzvah and now you're a man. There's a world to Judaism that is not quite so profoundly understood in America today. That's my sense.

ANDY: When we were little, we would sing and dance for guests. And there was no embarrassment. There was no sense of self-consciousness. But at our bar mitzvah, there was the beginning of a sense of self-consciousness. Where you're very aware of how you look and what other people might think.

I think the bar mitzvah marks a transition not just spiritually or in terms of religion, but also psychologically. And for me, I think that the value of that rite of passage was to be aware of myself as a boy becoming a man in a Jewish tradition and also in a modern, more just consciousness-based sense.

Looking back at my bar mitzvah now, I have a lot of memories of my childhood. The joke in our family is I got all the memory cells. I remember from the age of two on. Josh doesn't remember last week. I can look back and see my childhood memories as different in some way than what took place from thirteen on. So it really is an amazing point of change, I think, in a boy's or a girl's life. It's hard to think about who am I, what is this? What is my culture about? How do these traditions affect me personally? What is this that I'm actually saying here in this language? And how am I different from this point on? So looking back, I can see life before my bar mitzvah. It was a more innocent and unreflective period. And then starting from the bar mitzvah, I really started thinking about who am I and how do I fit into the world.

JOSH: Is your consciousness changing from a psychological perspective because of your age or because of the catalyst of the actual bar mitzvah?

ANDY: I would say more because of the age. I don't think the bar mitzvah was placed at thirteen arbitrarily. We had events when we were much younger that could have been seen as just as challenging from a performance perspective, where we would do Gilbert and Sullivan routines for guests that we didn't know. And we'd run around and sing. We'd do *Pirates of Penzance.* It was the Josh and Andy Show every Friday, when we had guests over for Shabbat. And we never thought twice about it. And if you look at young children who sing and dance, they don't think twice about it. They play in the bathtub. They're not thinking, "Oh, I'm naked." They play with their friends in the park, and they're not thinking about how they appear, until they hit a certain age. And I think that it's traditional, the young adult, twelve-, thirteen-year-old time period, where girls start to become very aware of how they're perceived in their peer groups, boys start to act very differently. And I think that part of why the bar mitzvah is so resonant and important a symbol is because it happens at the right time period.

IF EITHER OF YOU COULD DO IT AGAIN AT EIGHTY-THREE, LIKE KIRK DOUGLAS, WOULD YOU HAVE ANOTHER BAR MITZVAH?

ANDY: We did it in part because everyone was doing it at that time. We just didn't question it. When someone does it as an adult, it really marks a greater conscious commitment. You're not going through it with a thirteen-year-old mind. You're going through it with a mature mind. Our mother was bat mitzvahed, though, a few years ago. She was probably fifty-five. She did it on her own. She learned how to read the haftarah. I think she just took so much pride in our combined bar mitzvah ceremony and wished that she had had one. But for her to do it in her fifties is a testament to her and shows the importance of Judaism in her life. She lived vicariously through us when it was our turn. But it wasn't enough; she wanted to have her own experience of what it meant to stand there. It was also at Park Avenue Synagogue, and she was on the same bimah as we were on. We were so proud.

Josh: She's the embodiment of Judaism in the Bernstein family. For her to have her sons bar mitzvahed was sort of nonnegotiable. And then for her to physically do it herself was a huge milestone. It was probably one of the greatest moments, one of the top three, in her life.

WHAT TYPE OF TRADITIONS WILL YOU HAVE WITH YOUR FAMILY WHEN AND IF YOU HAVE CHILDREN, AND WILL THE BAR AND BAT MITZVAH BE AS PRIMARY AS IT WAS IN YOUR OWN LIFE?

Josh: You know, it's funny. After the year of study in Israel, most of the people in my class went on to rabbinical school. And I decided to go do desert survival and get back involved with BOSS, which is now the company that I own and run. I think that for me, Judaism is all about family.

But I do believe there is spiritual importance that I won't ignore in my life. I view Judaism as one path to the top of the mountain, and Christianity is another path, and Buddhism is another path. And there's no one path that's better than the others, because we're all trying to get to the top. But Judaism is a very distinct and difficult path. It always has been.

DID YOU EVER THINK THAT YOU WANTED TO BE A RABBI?

Josh: Oh, sure. I went and I looked at JTS [Jewish Theological Seminary]. I considered rabbinical school very seriously. But—

Andy: That's where the beard started.

Josh: That's where the beard started.

ANDY: He had a beard, a bigger beard.

JOSH: I did want to be a rabbi when I was younger. It was right after my year of study.

ANDY: I don't remember ever aspiring to be a rabbi. I didn't spend a year in Israel [as] Josh did. What I love most about the Jewish spirit and the Jewish tradition is its questioning of the world and not taking anything for granted. I love really deeply investigating for yourself what does this mean, whether it's in the Talmud and the debates over Jewish meaning or Kabbalah, or the daily and weekly debates that take place in synagogues all over the world, where people ask themselves: Who am I? What are we doing here? What's important to me? How should I raise my family?

I think that of all the traditions one can be raised in, I'm proud to have been raised in a Jewish tradition, because it instilled in me a really deep love of questioning things in a way that's both scholarly and practical. And that will definitely play a part in my family life, when I have one, if I have one. Who knows?

But whether or not it's manifested in symbols like the bar mitzvah, I think there would be a conversation initially with my future wife and then with our children, and their thoughts about life. I would want them to question everything. And if they do and we do feel that this particular rite of passage has value for them, I would totally embrace that.

JOSH: Whereas I would definitely have my child bar mitzvahed.

HOW WAS IT TO SHARE IN THIS AS TWINS?

ANDY: I love that I was bar mitzvahed with Josh, because I was less scared. We could practice together. Every time we had to go see the cantor and practice our haftarah portion, we were always on the same page. We shared the same schedule. We shared the same experiences. So for me—and this is the case in so many ways in my life—having had Josh along with the same experiences and often the same perspective on things, it's always made the experience richer.

I think that the bar mitzvah actually turned out to be where we started as individuals, splitting off a little bit. Up till then, it was basically the Josh and Andy Show. And we did everything together. We even wore some of the same clothes, just different colors.

And shortly after that, our father died. And Josh's interest in exploring his world went external, and he would go off to the West to ride horses and live out his adventures and ex-

ANDY (LEFT) AND JOSH AT THE BAR MITZVAH PARTY

plore his world. And I became more internal and turned toward psychology and understanding the mind. And I think looking back, if you were to trace our paths and how they've diverged just from the outsider's perspective, it was really around the time of our bar mitzvah which marked the turning point for us to start looking at what made us *us*.

JOSH: I also think that it's interesting to see now how Andy and I are both very individual and self-confident and motivated, ambitious people. But at the same time, there is that yin and yang aspect. When I was a kid and I had those summers on ranches or scuba diving or mountain climbing, I would come back and bring those adventures to the household, and Andy and I would live through each other's adventures vicariously. It's sort of like we get twice as much done in the same amount of time. There's an unusual bond. I don't pretend to be Andy and he doesn't pretend to be me. But we can share each other's experiences in a way that people who aren't twins wouldn't get.

ANDY: And I think that the bar mitzvah was one of the last great shared experiences we had as a team. Now we'll get together for birthdays and do some things together when we're in the same part of the world. But up until thirteen, we really did everything together. It was the Bernstein twins.

After our bar mitzvah is when we started thinking, Well, I don't want to have a Bernstein twins party. I want to have my own friends and my own party. So that was really the last great hurrah of being a child. And after that and then our father's death the following year, it was really the beginning of another stage in our lives. I think that the significance of the ceremony, of the bar mitzvah and bat mitzvah ceremony as a symbol, is that it makes that transition visual and tangible for kids and their parents. We recognize that something's changing there, and the ceremony celebrates that.

JOSH: I think there's more to it. I'm the one who studied mysticism and understood the magic of the words in the Bible. I think that being asked to partake in this tradition that goes back thousands of years across hundreds of generations, and to be able to read from the same scroll and to wear the traditions of Judaism and step into that role, is more than just a practical reading of texts.

There is a spiritual change that happens in someone when they become bar mitzvahed. And just because someone may not have that perspective when they're twelve or thirteen doesn't mean they should avoid or ignore it or miss out on it. Because when you're later inducted into that perspective and you realize, "Wow, tradition does mean a lot. I am part of this—it's critical."

That's why I think Kirk Douglas and people who do or redo this later in life think, Wow! I'm going to do that, That's why mother said, "I'm going to do that, because I missed out on an aspect of this culture that is transformative, practically as well as spiritually." There's meaning there.

Marlee Matlin

She's an Oscar-winning actress, a mother of four, and for Marlee Matlin, her bat mitzvah was a turning point in her life. Matlin lost her hearing at the age of eighteen months, but that didn't stop her from doing what she wanted to do. At the age of seven, she was Dorothy in a Chicago children's theater group's production of *The Wizard of Oz.* She attended Harper College, where she studied criminal justice, and while there rediscovered her passion for acting. After appearing in a local Chicago production of the Tony Award–winning play *Children of a Lesser God,* she starred in the movie version and won the Best Actress Oscar for her performance. This was her first film. With the film *Walker,* which was shot in Nicaragua, Marlee Matlin began visiting hearing and nonhearing children in communities worldwide.

Her academic work in criminal justice came in handy for her work in the 1991 television series *Reasonable Doubts,* in which she played an assistant district attorney. She was an Emmy Award nominee for her work on *Picket Fences, Seinfeld, The Practice* and *Law & Order: Special Victims Unit.* Most recently, she played Marlee the Librarian in *Blues Clues,* Nickelodeon's Emmy Award–winning show and starred for seven years on the award-winning *The West Wing.*

Matlin's first novel for children, *Deaf Child Crossing,* is loosely based on her own childhood in Chicago, and it inspired two more novels published by Simon & Schuster. In a key real-life role, she helped get a law passed forcing television manufacturers to place a chip enabling closed-captioning for the hearing impaired on all television screens larger than thirteen inches. She continued her work in this area, serving as the national spokesperson for the biggest closed-captioning provider. Giving back to the community is Marlee Matlin's passion. She is a national celebrity spokesperson for the American Red Cross and serves on the boards of Easter Seals and the Children Affected by Aids Foundation. In addition to her hard work and dedication, she also has a wonderful sense of humor and particularly enjoys reading lips "when the words are bleeped out on television."

Marlee Matlin is married to Kevin Grandalski and has four children—Sarah, Brandon, Tyler and Isabelle.

TEARS OF JOY THAT WILL LEAVE
THEIR MARK FOREVER

When the doctors realized I was deaf and said to my parents, when I was eighteen months old, that I should be sent to an institution hundreds of miles away from home, my parents said, "No, we want Marlee to be with us. It's about family and it's about saying I love you every night and we don't want to send her away." That was important to them because that's what a Jewish household is all about. It's about family. And there's also an aspect of Judaism that says, "You know what? We don't necessarily want to do it your way. We want to do it our way." When it came to my being bat mitzvahed at thirteen, most people would have questioned the decision to go ahead. My parents found a temple in Chicago, Temple Bene Shalom, that had a congregation that included both hearing and deaf people. The rabbi there, Rabbi Douglas Goldhammer, could sign. It was pretty unusual, to see a girl who was deaf being bat mitzvahed. I was able to do it because my parents had that "We don't care what people think. Let's just do it" attitude.

And that's the kind of thing I passed along to my children, that sense of independence, a sense of "Okay, so it may take you forty years to get to Israel, but at least you get there." So it may be a little bit more difficult to raise a child who happens to be hearing impaired, but you get it done. And I'm always fortunate and thankful every day.

NEEDLESS TO SAY, YOUR BAT MITZVAH WAS CHALLENGING FOR YOU.

Yes, learning Hebrew was one of the hardest things I'd ever had to do. I didn't have the benefit of hearing myself say the words. So I had to phonetically learn how to pronounce them. At the ceremony I was saying my haftarah and I was pronouncing the words. I may not have gotten the tune right because obviously, being deaf, you can't hear the music. But I could hear the words in my head. I learned to pronounce the words. And when I looked up from my haftarah as I was reading, I saw my parents crying. I thought, Oh my gosh, I'm doing something wrong, and I started to cry. I found out later that they weren't crying, of course, because I was doing something wrong. They were crying out of happiness. And so I finished, and I was so happy that I had gotten through it while everybody was crying.

Then I looked down and I realized that I had cried on the Torah parchment. There were tears on the Torah parchment. I was mortified. And the rabbi said afterward, "Marlee, you know, your tears are a mitzvah." And I couldn't figure that out. He said, "Because most times in Jewish history when we think about bad things that have happened, they're always accompanied by tears. In this case, we have a Torah with your tearstains, but they represent this wonderful event that happened in the community, which is your becoming a part of the Jewish community. And you are a bat mitzvah. And how wonderful that we have these tearstains to remind us of the wonderful thing that you've done." What Rabbi Goldhammer said to me always stuck with me.

YOUR BAT MITZVAH SERVICE WAS SO EMOTIONAL AND TOUCHING. I WOULD IMAGINE YOUR FRIENDS WERE VERY SUPPORTIVE OF YOU.

I had a lot of friends there. Half my friends there were deaf and half were hearing. I was thirteen years old, but I had been an actress since I was seven, and it was almost like being on stage. I wasn't afraid. I wanted to make sure I got everything right. We had a nice ceremony. My parents were there and my family was there and my friends were there. But I didn't have a boyfriend until I was fifteen.

My best friend, Liz Tannebaum, who was also deaf, was there. We actually met in Sunday school. I was five and she was six. And I said, "I'll be your best friend," and she said, "I'll be your best friend." And we celebrated my bat mitzvah together. She was always there for me. And it was a wonderful experience to have her there with me, and it was important for me to have that best friend there by my side supporting me the whole way.

A bar or bat mitzvah is about a couple of things. First, it's about developing discipline. You have to go every week to Hebrew school and study your Hebrew. Secondly, it's about appreciation of who you are and your roots. A bat or bar mitzvah is important because it gives children a sense of community and a sense of belonging, which I think is a big thing that's lacking these days in children. My husband is a police officer. And we always talk about why there are so many kids in gangs these days and what are the causes of this behavior. Personally, I think the behavior results from kids feeling like they have no place to go or a place to belong. I think all kids just feel a need to be part of something, whether it's a family or church, a temple or a school.

Plus you get lots of nice gifts! It is just a wonderful thing for a kid to go through. It's a coming of age, a rite of passage. I can't imagine any other activity at thirteen that's more fun. It's a great way to teach your children about community and social responsibility.

You know, Henry is one of the greatest influences in my life. When I was twelve, I was performing in Chicago at a benefit. Henry Winkler was there and I went right up to him and I said, "Hi, I'm Marlee and I want to be your best friend and I want to be an actor in Hollywood just like you."

And someone pulled Henry aside and said, "You better not encourage her too much because, you know, at the end of the day she's not going to really be able to get a chance to work in Hollywood. And you wouldn't want to disappoint a young girl, would you?" And Henry sort of nodded his head.

Then he turned around and he kneeled down and he said to me, "You know, Marlee, sweetheart, you can do whatever you want to do. What people are telling me to tell you is the same thing that people told me. And I only got to where I was because I followed my heart. The only way you can get to where you are is to follow your heart and not let people say that you can't. Just do what you think you can do." Nine years after that, when I won the Oscar, I went to his house and showed him the Oscar and said, "Look what I got, Henry."

The day after I won the Oscar, Rex Reed wrote in the newspaper that I won out of pity and that I didn't deserve an Oscar because I didn't say a word. And that I would never work in Hollywood again because I'm deaf. I said, "Henry, what do I do?" And Henry said, "Marlee, the same advice applies now as it did when you were twelve. Don't pay attention to anybody. Just follow your heart and do whatever you want. Your dreams will come true. Come and stay with us for the weekend and we'll help sort it out for you." And so I stayed in Henry and Stacey Winkler's guesthouse. And interestingly, that weekend turned into a week and then it turned into a month. I ended up living at the Winkler house for two years. I became their unofficial fourth child. Stacey Winkler taught me how to make a wonderful brisket. Henry was great because he would screen all my dates. He would be there at the door with his little checklist making sure that all my dates were appropriate. I ended up getting married on the front lawn of his house.

MARLEE WITH HER DAUGHTER ISABELLE, AGE TWO

AND YOU ALSO GREW UP TO BE INCREDIBLY SUCCESSFUL, NOT TO MENTION AN OSCAR-
WINNER. YOU MUST FEEL TERRIBLY BLESSED.

I learned from that newspaper experience I had that you can't get complacent. People are still going to have preconceived notions about you. Now, if somebody says, "Marlee, you're great, you've broken down barriers," I say, "No, I haven't broken down barriers. I've just learned to walk around them and keep walking in a straight line. Breaking down barriers is for, you know, politicians, and about fighters. I don't consider myself a fighter so much as I am just somebody who wants and deserves respect just like anybody else.

Henry Winkler

Henry passed on a chance to labor in the lumber business. If acting didn't work out, his plans were to become a child psychologist. Lucky for us it did, and as a result, "The Fonz" will live on forever.

Henry Winkler was born and raised on the Upper West Side of Manhattan. Little did anyone know at the time, but Henry was dyslexic. He struggled through school but eventually overcame his learning disability, and then some.

Henry Winkler graduated from Emerson College in 1967 and received his Master of Fine Arts from the Yale School of Drama in 1970. Then, in 1978, he earned a PhD in Hebrew Literature from Emerson College.

His interest in acting had developed early, around the time he won the leading role in his school play, *Billy Budd,* when he was in the eighth grade. After Yale, he found work in commercials, and in 1974, he got his first major film role in *The Lords of Flatbush.* Also in 1974, when Henry Winkler was twenty-seven years old, he became Arthur "Fonzie" ("The Fonz") Fonzarelli in the television series *Happy Days,* on ABC. The character became an icon, the epitome of cool, and won his way into households across the country. Ratings zoomed sky-high thanks to Fonzie's popularity. But Winkler is also famous for remaining levelheaded during his rise to celebrity.

After ten years, *Happy Days* was canceled and Henry Winkler went on to producing and directing a multitude of projects. He also appeared in films: *Night Shift, Scream, The Waterboy,* and *Holes.* Winkler found roles in television episodes of *The Practice, Crossing Jordan,* and *Arrested Development* and starred in *Out of Practice.* In *Happy Days: 30th Anniversary Reunion* (2005), he had two roles, one off screen as executive producer and the other as The Fonz. His performance in the PBS children's animated series *Clifford's Puppy Days* earned him the 2004–2005 Daytime Emmy Award. Broadway audiences were lucky to watch him in *The Dinner Party,* a Neil Simon play.

Using his experience with dyslexia as a theme, Henry Winkler has coauthored a

children's book series with Lin Oliver called *Hank Zipzer: The World's Best Under-achiever.*

Henry Winkler and his wife, Stacey, are involved with several charities. They founded the Children's Action Network, which gives free immunizations to more than 200,000 children. Other organizations benefiting from the Winkler's devotion to helping others are the MacLaren Children's Center, the National Committee for Arts for the Handicapped, the Los Angeles Music Center's Very Special Arts Festival, and the Special Olympics.

Henry and Stacey Winkler have three children.

HENRY AND HIS SISTER, BEA, WITH THEIR PARENTS, ILSE AND HARRY

THIRTEEN WAS *AAAAYYYY* GREAT YEAR

I had my bar mitzvah on November 8, 1958, at Congregation Habonim on West 66th Street between Central Park West and Broadway in Manhattan. It was our neighborhood synagogue and not far from where we lived at 78th and Broadway.

It's no coincidence that the character that I write about in my books lives in my old building, goes to P.S.87, which is down the street, and has learning challenges just like I did. I'm dyslexic, which is a real problem when you're trying to read and a huge problem when you're studying Hebrew. I learned my haftarah phonetically because there was no way I was learning Hebrew. I was having enough trouble reading English from left to right. Reading Hebrew from right to left and dealing with those letters that I couldn't figure out for all the tea in China was too much for me. It was so difficult because everybody else was reading from the prayer book and the Torah. And I was struggling. I had to memorize it like I was playing a part. Not much was known about dyslexia at the time so I was labeled lazy and inattentive. It was confusing to me because I knew I was smart, but for some reason I didn't understand the reading.

CONSIDERING YOU HAVE DYSLEXIA, I WOULD IMAGINE LEARNING THE HEBREW PORTION MUST HAVE BEEN DIFFICULT FOR YOU.

I was a nervous wreck. At the service, you have to read your haftarah portion in Hebrew and then you have to read the story in English. This was really hard for me. The words would just swim around on the page. In fact, I did not actually read a novel until the eleventh or twelfth grade in high school. My bar mitzvah was a real milestone for me because I was tackling the ultimate challenge. What I remember is that I got mixed up. I did the second prayer first. So I just had to stop and start again. The rabbi looked at me. I looked at him and I just went, "Well, what can I do?" And I went back and started again.

I was definitely not comfortable being in front of a crowd. Now, I speak publicly across the country quite comfortably, but when I started, I would be in a panic. In my late twenties I thought that being an actor was like being a brain surgeon. When you're fifty-five, you finally get it all together. Only now am I relaxing into getting better. It was different for me at thirteen. I didn't really like it all that much.

At that time, all I thought was, Am I ever going to get through this? The Torah portion was relatively short but I felt like I had been reading from the Torah for about a month and a half. It just wouldn't end. I don't remember how many people were there or whether the party was good or not, but I do remember the reading part and how tough it was. And I remember that the party was at the Alcott Hotel on West 72nd Street. I remember that I got one of those first Polaroid cameras that folded down and you pulled it all the way out. Then you had to wait sixty seconds, and then you had to peel the picture away from the chemical. I also remember that I could really dance. I did the limbo and a modified Kazatski, the Russian dance where they kick their legs out. I was not a good reader, but I was a good mover.

DID YOU FEEL AT THAT POINT THAT YOU WERE A MAN?

I felt like I barely fit in the suit, but I did have really great loafers. They were square-toed. I always had to wear sensible shoes. My parents escaped from Nazi Germany and were frugal. The soap we used my mother usually took from hotels when we were on vacation. Everything is different today, I know. My bar mitzvah was different from what they are today. Now, there's too much pressure for the parents to have their child's celebration measure up, and it must be excruciating for the child when their bar mitzvah is not as extravagant as their friends'. It's not even healthy, let alone fun.

It's a five-thousand-year-old tradition. When you stand up there, there is a sense of this continuum that you are aware of even at thirteen. That's big. However, if you have to have a ship sail across the dance floor to bring in the bar or bat mitzvah boy or girl, do they get the real meaning of the ritual?

My bar mitzvah was an accomplishment. I'm very proud that I went through it. And I'm very proud that I then continued it as a parent with my own children, who, by the way, are all dyslexic. It's hereditary. But they did a fantastic job, my children. Once I understood that they had my problem, I never again said to my son, "You can't do your homework with the radio playing," because I finally realized that the music might be helping him focus.

YOU'RE VERY SIMILAR TO THE CHARACTER WHO MADE YOU FAMOUS, "THE FONZ." HE HAD SENSITIVITY WITH A SENSE OF HUMOR. DID YOU HAVE THAT SENSE OF HUMOR AT THIRTEEN?

Yes, but I think I did it with timing. I didn't feel funny although I was a class clown. I was social, a gadfly. I would show up at a school dance or a temple dance and I had to make sure that I talked to every human being in the place, that I had somehow to make the rounds. I couldn't relax. Some people, especially the girls, found me too intense, to tell you the truth. And not only that, but if I was stupid enough to take a date to one of these dances, she would spend a lot of time by herself because I had to make contact with everybody. It was a compulsion. Interestingly enough, The Fonz was my alter ego. He was everybody I wanted to be but wasn't. I wasn't even close to being the cool guy that every girl wanted to be with. I had a lot of braces on my teeth, thanks to Dr. Murray Zimmerman. My mouth was full of metal and rubber bands.

HENRY AND BEA

A lot. He was a cool guy but there were times when he wasn't. He would be at home, with his jacket off, and there was no one to be cool for. He was left with himself. There had to be that emotional side to him. My learning disabilities were also a part of The Fonz. He was cool, but he wasn't the straight-A student.

YOUR PARENTS ARE HOLOCAUST SURVIVORS. DID YOUR BAR MITZVAH HAVE MORE MEANING TO YOU BECAUSE OF THAT?

I don't think so. I think it had an incredible amount of meaning to me because I believe that no matter how much children fight it, there is a sense of extraordinary pride in each child. We just went to a bat mitzvah and the girl, who is usually shy and stays out of the limelight, stood there and she was in charge.

Sometimes, as an adult, you see these children up on the bima and you see a vision of who they will be, taking on this extraordinary responsibility and this extraordinary challenge that they meet. I watched all three of my children up there, my two boys and my one girl. You know who they are at home and you know how fresh they are and how sassy. And all of a sudden you see them taking on the mantle of this responsibility. It's so touching, I don't know what to do. There is so much joy in seeing them go through this. And you know what I love? I love that for five thousand years people have tried to destroy the Jewish culture and we're still here and we're still relevant. And we're still contributors to the world everywhere.

Ed Koch

Ed Koch, a registered Democrat and a practicing Jew, served as the 105th mayor of New York City for three terms, from 1978 through 1989. In the 1981 election, he ran as both a Democrat and a Republican, endorsed by both parties and proud of his Jewish heritage. His career in New York City politics began in 1963 when he was elected Democratic district leader of Greenwich Village. The "How'm I doing?" former mayor is a native New Yorker and grew up in the Bronx and Newark, New Jersey, where he graduated from South Side High School. He attended City College of New York and graduated from New York University Law School in 1948. Mayor Koch is famous for having kept New York City from going bankrupt in the late 1970s and putting the city on a balanced budget for the first time in fifteen years. He gave the city back its spirit, created two hundred fifty thousand affordable housing units, and put in place a judicial merit system in the selection of Criminal and Family Court judges.

After serving as mayor, Ed Koch joined the law firm of Robinson, Silverman, Pearce, Aronsohn, and Berman LLP, now Bryan Cave LLP, as partner. He is also an author and has written eight political books: *Mayor, Politics, His Eminence and Hizzoner, All the Best, Citizen Koch, Ed Koch on Everything, Guiliani: Nasty Man,* and *I'm Not Done Yet: Remaining Relevant.* He coauthored two children's books with his sister, Pat Koch Thaler: *Eddie, Harold's Little Brother* and *Eddie's Little Sister Makes a Splash.* In addition, two current books to be published are *Buzz* (2007), coauthored by Christy Heady, and *Confronting Anti-Semitism & The Holocaust* (2008), coauthored by Rafael Medoff.

Ed Koch is a political commentator on television and radio and writes a weekly political column, along with movie reviews. The multitasking Ed Koch became a judge on *The People's Court* for two years on television and an adjunct professor at New York University for several years. He performed in an episode of *Sex and the City,* and appeared in a number of Hollywood films. He is one of the first mayors ever to host *Saturday Night Live.*

ED WITH HIS SISTER, PAT

HOW'M I DOING?
AICH ANI OSE?

My bar mitzvah stands out as a major event in my life. We had the ceremony at the Ohev Sholom Synagogue on High Street in Newark, New Jersey. Having a bar mitzvah is an important milestone, a tradition. You prepare for it at the synagogue. They teach you the section of the Torah that you're going to read and the section of the haftarah. In those days, you were expected to make a speech thanking your mother and father, which I did. We were low middle class or worse in those days. I didn't have a catered bar mitzvah. We had the party in our house. I suspect about a hundred people were there, relatives and friends. I remember that my sister, who is now a grandmother, was about five years old at the time. My mother did the cooking. My parents, Joyce Silpe Koch and Louis Koch, were both immigrants coming from Poland in the early 1900s, when Poland was a province of the Austrian-Hungarian Empire.

YOUR BAR MITZVAH GAVE YOU A FORUM IN WHICH TO SPEAK. WERE YOU ANXIOUS? DID YOU FEEL THEN THAT YOU COULD GROW UP TO BE A GREAT ORATOR?

No, it would be silly to think that only one instance of speaking in front of a crowd is something that would have a special impact on my ability to speak in public forums. Also, I have no doubt that I was anxious. I don't speak Hebrew now and didn't back then. I learned it by rote and I know that I wanted to do a good job. I felt the pressure.

And today, I'm a very proud Jew, proud to have been bar mitzvahed, and conscious of the traditions of my religion. I think that the people in New York City know that I was desirous of making clear to people when I was mayor that I was a Jew, treating other Jews no better or no worse than anybody else in this city. I'm proud of my people's accomplishment historically and in New York and in the United States.

GROWING UP, DID OTHER KIDS YOU KNOW HAVE BAR MITZVAHS?

I would say that everybody in the area of Newark where I grew up was Jewish and all the boys had bar mitzvahs. None of them are around anymore. Some are dead and some moved away from the New York area.

WHAT ABOUT NOW? DO YOU STILL ATTEND BAR MITZVAHS?

In our family, the first bat mitzvah of a granddaughter, my sister's granddaughter, was held in California about two or three years ago. And we went out there to participate and be with her at the time. It's lovely to see both the bar mitzvahs and the bat mitzvahs. We're looking forward to the first bar mitzvah, of Noah, who is my sister's grandchild and the son of her son, Jon.

YOU TAKE PRIDE IN YOUR RELIGION. WHAT ARE THE QUALITIES AND THE TRADITIONS THAT MAKE YOU MOST PROUD TO BE JEWISH?

I believe that Jews have achieved great success not only in the United States, but throughout the world. But we are and should be particularly grateful to the United States for its openness to the Jewish community and its very small anti-Semitic population. We have a lot to thank the United States for. And I do that every day. I think about it.

On Rosh Hashanah of this year, 5767, I attended services as I have done for the last forty years at the Park East Synagogue in Manhattan. Since I left the mayoralty some seventeen years ago, Rabbi Arthur Schneier has asked me to speak to the congregation on Rosh Hashanah, marking the beginning of the new year. This year, I focused on the incredible upheaval happening in the world today. I also spoke about Daniel Pearl, the *Wall Street Journal* reporter who was taken hostage by the terrorists in Pakistan. They paraded him on television and forced him to say, "My father is Jewish, my mother is Jewish, I am Jewish." Then they slit his throat and decapitated him with the world watching the video of the murder.

That morning the rabbi told us of the importance of the prayers we recite on Rosh Hashanah and that we should be conscious of their special significance. I hope that someday soon we will add Daniel Pearl's words to a special prayer. "My father is Jewish, my mother is Jewish, I am Jewish."

My speech was well received by the synagogue. In fact, they applauded, which is very unusual in a synagogue.

Bark Mitzvah Lady
with
Arthur and Murray

They called Ruth Bell's boys tall, dark and handsome, and indeed they were, with their muscular bodies, sleek black fur and glistening eyes. Standing a statuesque eighteen inches tall, top to toe, the elegantly craggy-faced guys were a dynamic drooling duo. They grew up in New York City and in the Hamptons, and happily divided their time between the two places, always accompanied by their loving adoptive mother, Ruth Bell. Arthur and Murray expected nothing but the best from life, and boy, did they get it when Ruth threw them a spectacular double "*bark* mitzvah," and that's no typo.

Being popular pups, Arthur and Murray relished their dog and people friends (the people friends came to their "bark mitzvah"), but who did they like spending time with most of all besides their mother? Each other. They loved each other and were loyal to the end. When Murray fell into the pool, Arthur found Ruth and indicated through barking that his brother was in deep trouble. Ruth jumped into the pool with her clothes on to finish the rescue Arthur had instigated. In their spare time, Arthur and Murray worked with what educators call *manipulatives*: bones and sometimes tennis balls. They craved their canned dog food and spurned the leftovers of people food. When they passed away, Ruth wasn't sure about having more but relented, and now has four loving dogs: Raymond Alexander, Duke, Lola May and Ella. (Raymond Alexander is named after Arthur and Lola May is named after Murray.) Arthur and Murray are buried together and share a headstone.

Ruth Bell, who is not losing it at all, grew up in Brooklyn. She graduated from Erasmus High School and the Fashion Institute of Technology. A Reform Jew, she did not have a bat mitzvah and did attend Hebrew school. Bell is involved with her local temple, the Hampton Synagogue, and started a scholarship fund named for her parents,

An annual party it has become
Let's share another evening of
food and fun !
Although this may seem a
a little hairy or furry
It's also a celebration for
Arthur and Murray!
A Bark Mitzvah reception
for the "Boys"
They will have read their Woof-
Torah with grace & poise
A Hora, a Brucha, and a
Candlelighting too!
Please join in this Simcha
Won't You?

ARTHUR (LEFT) AND MURRAY BELL

Irene and George Bell, to benefit the Hebrew school associated with the synagogue. Ruth Bell is a partner in the children's dance wear business, Ricki B. She enjoys everything, but especially spending time with her dogs, family and friends, in that order.

I met Ruth Bell at an event held by the Hadassah chapter in Westhampton. I had been chosen as the Hadassah Woman of the Year in 2005. During my talk, I mentioned this book project. Ruth Bell later called me with the details of Arthur and Murray's special day.

IT'S A DOG'S WORLD AFTER ALL

My dogs Arthur and Murray were "bark mitzvahed" on July 5, 1997, at my house in Quogue on Long Island. I had originally planned to take them to Israel, but it didn't work out. It would have been hard getting them in and out of the country. So I decided that we'd just have a good time here. I used to have a July Fourth party every year. And back then, in 1997, Arthur and Murray happened to be nearly two years old, which makes them thirteen in dog years. So I thought it would be a perfect time for a big celebration. Their birthday was September 1 so they were a solid thirteen at the time since technically one year for us is seven years for a dog, so they were thirteen going on fourteen. I know that everyone reading this will think I should be committed.

My friends thought it was the best party I ever had. I loved my dogs and I thought of them as my Jewish boys, although they weren't circumcised. We had a rabbi, a make-believe one. My rabbi, Rabbi Mark, said it was okay. He couldn't perform the ceremony himself because it was on a Saturday night. We had a bracha. Arthur and Murray, those good students, prepared. They had a practice ceremony with just a few select people in the morning. They read the Wolf Torah. This was the moment when they went from being puppies to dogs, in the Jewish religion.

At the real ceremony we had almost a hundred people. We invited people, not dogs, to this one. It wasn't kosher because Arthur and Murray were Reform. We had cocktails, hors d'oeuvres, dinner, and the *ha-motzi*, which is the prayer you say over the challah before you eat. Arthur and Murray stood up there during the *ha-motzi*. They ate the bread. And then we had a candle-lighting ceremony with thirteen or fourteen candles. We had matches that said "Arthur and Murray Bark Mitzvah. July 5th, 1997." At each table, everyone was given a candle to light. We had a wonderful cake that was shaped like a Torah. I read a poem. We had goody bags for the guests and T-shirts, too. The celebration was one of the highlights of my life.

It wasn't a real religious ceremony. It was a lark! We had a band and the party was catered. I called a caterer that I've used before and I said to him, "Myra, you're not going to believe what we're doing this year." And I said, "A 'bark mitzvah.'" She said, "A what?" So, I said, "You know my Arthur and Murray. It's time for them to be 'bark mitzvahed.'" I think she said to me, "Did you lose it?" I said, "No, I think I'm just getting it." It was all for my twin boys! This was nearly ten years ago, and I spent about ten thousand dollars on it. The celebration was intimate, at my house. If I had a son or daughter, there would have been a bar or bat mitzvah. Arthur and Murray, being dogs, got a "bark mitzvah."

My mother, may she rest in peace, would have been so proud of Moishe and Avram, which are their real Hebrew names. And they were proud, too. They're such big kosher

hams. The outfits they wore were rather formal and each had a tallis and yarmulke. The tables were designed especially with dogs in mind. The centerpieces were IAMS dog treat boxes filled with flowers. The tablecloths had pictures of hearts and dog bones. We had dancing. Arthur and Murray were great. I mean, they were very well behaved.

They got beautiful gifts, too, and they wrote thank-you notes signed with their paw prints. They got sterling silver Stars of David to wear on their collars. And they wore them. They got all kinds of leashes and food. Barbara Smith gave them a beautiful picnic basket complete with dog bowls. But they did not get any cash, which was fine because they didn't own any wallets.

DID YOU HAVE THE "BARK MITZVAH" BECAUSE YOU ARE RELIGIOUS OR JUST WANTED TO HAVE A PARTY FOR ARTHUR AND MURRAY?

Am I religious? Well, I like to eat. You know, that's what Jews do when they celebrate something, they eat. I had the "bark mitzvah" for Arthur and Murray because they're my kids. If had a son, I would have him bar mitzvahed. This is the same thing. They were entitled to this.

I'M ALMOST AFRAID TO ASK: WHAT ABOUT THEIR WEDDINGS?

I think they were gay. And anyhow, they are no longer alive. Arthur died first. He got hit by a car. I was in Atlanta at the time. I passed out when they told me. And my little Murray was blind. And he missed his brother, because his brother helped him around. Eventually, I had to put him down. It's never the right time. I buried each one with his tallis and yarmulke.

YOU STILL HAVE MANY DOGS, AND I'M TERRIFIED TO ASK, BUT WILL THEY HAVE "BARK MITZVAHS"?

I have four—Raymond, Dukie, Lola May and Ella. I was thinking of having a joint ceremony, but I don't know. I have to do four at one time because they're all the same age, the two girls and two boys. Or, I could wait and have Sweet Sixteens. And these dogs are straight, so there could be a chuppah in their future. My little Dukie has a crush on my big girl, Lola May. My dogs are my children. You know, if somebody says, "Well, could you get the dog out, you know, take the dogs outside?" I say, "No, they live here. You go outside. This is their house." My nephew and nieces were over a couple of weeks ago. They call me Tanta and one of them, Griffith, said, "Is Tanta rich?" So Cameron says, "She used to be, but she spends all her money on us and her dogs."

Judy Gold

Being Jewish and a mother is a formidable combination. Also an Emmy Award–winning actress and comedian, Judy Gold grew up in New Jersey, where she starred in her first one-woman show, her own bat mitzvah. Years later, her one-woman show, *25 Questions for a Jewish Mother,* would become a critically acclaimed Off-Broadway production.

As a child, Judy Gold didn't really fit in with the crowd. She was taller than the crowd, including her teachers, all the parents and the rabbi. Gold was also a musical child and enjoyed piano lessons and clarinet, which earned her the label Band Nerd. She attributes her height and her participation in the marching band and other musical outlets to her incredible lack of popularity among the teenage socialites in her New Jersey high school. Despite her lousy high school experience, Judy Gold always knew that her inner coolness would one day emerge. And it did, at Rutgers University, where she learned that she could make people laugh just by standing up and talking. After moving to New York City and finding work selling ad space, Gold bemoaned the fact that she was no longer doing stand-up as she had in college and she really missed it. Her friend Wendy finally got fed up and told Judy to either start doing stand-up again or quit talking about it. Thank you, Wendy, because we would have missed out on a major talent. We hope the newspapers found someone else to sell the ad space.

Gold is the host of HBO's *At the Multiplex with Judy Gold,* and also hosted Comedy Central's *100 Greatest Stand-ups of All Time* and the *GLADD Media Awards.* Her TV specials include a half-hour comedy special for LOGO and she is featured in the HBO documentary *All Aboard.* Her stand-up specials include *Comedy Central Presents: Judy Gold,* Comedy Central's *Tough Crowd Stands Up,* and Judy's HBO half-hour special, which received a Cable Ace Award. Gold also performed in the smash-hit film *The Aristocrats.* Other television appearances include *Law & Order, Law & Order: SVU, The View, The Tonight Show with Jay Leno,* and *Late Night with Conan O'Brien,* to name a few.

JUDY (SECOND FROM LEFT) WITH HER FAMILY

Gold won two Emmy Awards for writing and producing *The Rosie O'Donnell Show.* She was nominated twice for the American Comedy Awards' funniest female stand- up. *25 Questions for a Jewish Mother* earned Gold a nomination for a Drama Desk Award for Outstanding Solo Performance and won the 2007 GLAAD Media Award. A book based on the show was published earlier this year.

Gold lives in New York City with her two children. She frequently tours theaters and comedy clubs around the country. Her CD, *Judith's Roommate Had A Baby,* is available now. Check out www.JudyGold.com.

JUDY GOLD
REVENGE OF THE GIANT NERD

First, let's talk about my mother. She was born in 1922 and she wanted to attend Hebrew school, and since girls did not go to Hebrew school, she sat in on the classes voluntarily. When it was time for all the boys to be bar mitzvahed, they did a special service for my mother on Shavuos. They called it a confirmation, but in reality, it was actually one of the first bat mitzvahs ever because, back in 1935 there was no such thing. So my mother was really into the Jewy thing.

I grew up in Clark, New Jersey, and we were members of Temple Beth O'r. I went to Hebrew school, but mostly I hated it and thought it was really boring. I did enjoy going to synagogue, especially because on Friday nights after the service they served these really good brownies. We went pretty much every week after Shabbos dinner. We went for every holiday. We even made a sukkah in our backyard. We were very kosher. I would consider us Jewy Jews. For me, becoming a bat mitzvah wasn't even a choice. My brother had a bar mitzvah, and my parents just had a little luncheon at the house afterward. My sister had a bat mitzvah on a Friday night and then my parents just had dessert afterward.

Everyone else had these *huge* friggin' parties, right? *Huge,* like . . . I remember the first bat mitzvah of my year, the service was on Friday night and on Saturday night was the big shindig. And my mother—I was six feet tall—my mother made me a dress. She had to make a lot of my clothes because I was so tall. So she made me this dress, a jumper that came down to my knees, so I arrive at my first big bat mitzvah and I'm the only one in a short dress and I'm six feet tall. Everyone else was wearing these long gowns. And you know how they would seat you a the kids' table? Well, here's how it worked. Depending on how popular you were, that's how close you got to sit to the bat mitzvah girl. So there I was, not only in a short dress, but I was seated with her little cousins at the end of the second tier. From that point on I made my mom buy me a long gown for all the big bar mitzvah parties.

Months later, I had high hopes for my own bat mitzvah. I was looking forward to picking out the party favors we would give to the kids. Everyone would give these huge gifts. You'd get picture frames, caricatures, dolls, paperweights, country homes—you name it. Now, my mother was very traditional, and thought that the religious aspect of the bat mitzvah was the most significant. So when she said to me, "I'll give you a dinner before, and they can have coffee and dessert afterward," needless to say, I was distressed. I thought "Uuhhhh, I'm already unpopular and *NOW* you're going to make me even *more unpopular*!" My sister was very artistic and she handmade the invitations. I couldn't have been from a nerdier family. You know, everyone else has bows and the raised lettering and I have my sister doing calligraphy. They had them printed and then she hand-painted each one. I mean, now that I think back, it was nice, but at the time I thought it was horrible.

Still, I looked forward to it. I was excited because I would get to perform. Because of my height, I was the only kid who didn't have to stand on a platform. I was even taller than the rabbi. I did my haftarah and I was perfect. I wore an orange dress, although there are no pictures because my mother wouldn't use a camera in the synagogue on Shabbos. Basically, we had our dinner, and then I did the service and then we had dessert, and that was it. Isn't that so boring?

But I did get gifts and money. My parents took it and put it all in a bank account for me. And of course, I was such a nerd, and I played the clarinet, and when I was a junior in high school I had to have the BEST clarinet!! And I took the money and bought a really expensive clarinet. Which of course I still have but never play.

DID YOU AT LEAST PUT THE CLARINET TO GOOD USE AT THE BAT MITZVAH PARTY?

Oh God, no. The party was at the synagogue. There was no music. On a scale of one to ten, I would say it was a two. Everyone just ate dinner. There was no big dessert table. I remember that at one bat mitzvah, the bat mitzvah girl came out of a cake . . . with sparklers! At mine we had party favors that my mother picked out. For the girls, there were little change purses with a paisley design, and key chains for the boys. So I said, "Ma, I've got old parents, I'm six feet tall, and these are the gifts. Can't we at least have the velvet yarmulkes?" Her answer was, "No, the plain ones," and I just thought, Oh God!

DOES THAT EXPLAIN WHY YOU BECAME THE PERSON YOU ARE NOW? AND THAT YOU BECAME A COMEDIAN BECAUSE OF YOUR CHILDHOOD?

Yes, I mean back then I wanted to kill her, but she really did teach me good values, I think. Despite my feelings at the time, my kids go to Hebrew school and I observe many of the tenets that I love about the religion. I see the value of observing Shabbos on Friday night. The fact that my mother did adhere to the traditions and didn't get into this whole battle about "Okay, we're going to have the biggest party" is quite meaningful to me now. I do thank her for that.

Recently, I was at my mother's house and I was going to pick up some sandwiches at the deli. Before I left to go pick up the food, she said, "Wait, let me give you the money," and she pulled out her wallet and she gave me some cash. As I was walking away she said, "Wait, let me give you some change," and then she pulled out the change purse from my bat mitzvah thirty-one years before.

OH MY GOODNESS, DON'T TELL ME YOUR FATHER STILL HAD THE KEYCHAIN . . .

No, he's dead.

WELL, HE MAY STILL HAVE THE KEYCHAIN . . .

Yeah, it's probably in the coffin. I'm telling you, I said, "Mom, it's bad enough that you have macaroni art on your dresser . . . but it's unbelievable that you still have that stupid little change purse from the bat mitzvah."

FOR MANY PEOPLE IN THIS BOOK THIS SPECIAL CELEBRATION WAS A REAL TURNING POINT IN THEIR LIVES. DID YOU FEEL THAT WAY?

Oh yeah, I couldn't wait to make my speech! And I was going to sing that haftarah because, you know, there was no way I was ever going to be an ingenue. I'm six feet tall, and I'm a nerd. This was the *HERE I AM!!!* moment. I'm going to sing my haftarah and you're going to hear it and *I'M THE STAR!!!* And then I'm going give my speech and you're all going to listen. I was so looking forward to it and I was determined not to make any mistakes. It was like I was the star in the school play—and that certainly wasn't going to happen.

What being up there showed me is that there was something in me that knew that I was not a loser. I got teased a lot and I was not in the cool crowd at all and most of the kids were really nasty. I can't exactly pinpoint what it was, but I had some kind of drive that got me through it. There was something deep down inside me that knew I wasn't a loser at all.

DID THAT WACKY HUMOR OF YOURS COME OUT?

I definitely had a sense of humor at the time, but since I don't remember what I said in my speech I don't know if it had any funny parts. I think the only humorous bit was that the rabbi was five foot two, and I'm standing there the six-foot-tall bat mitzvah girl.

YOU SAID YOU WERE *NOT* POPULAR IN SCHOOL . . .

Not at all. I stood out like a sore thumb. Actually, I grew up and went to Hebrew school with this one clique of girls, and they were the really popular girls. This is one of my favorite stories. It was the protocol that you invited everyone in your Hebrew school class to your bar or bat mitzvah even if you weren't friends with them. So, one Saturday morning, we were all at a bar mitzvah, and I'm sitting there with everyone else, and one of the popular girls comes in and starts pointing, to each kid and says, "Did you get my invitation?" Then she points to me doesn't say a word, and skips to the next person. Now how mean is that?

I THINK YOU SHOULD SEND HER AN INVITATION TO YOUR SHOW AND SAY, "LOOK AT ME NOW."

That's right! She can pay sixty-five dollars to see my ass up there! The funny thing is that growing up, the two things I hated the most were going to the temple with the clique of Jews and going to high school. I hated both of those places. Last year the temple really needed to raise money, and so who did they call and ask to do a fund-raiser? And so I ended up doing this show at the damn high school! I got on stage and did a benefit for the synagogue at my old high school.

My whole show is about my being a Jew, being gay, being a mother and being a daughter. I think of myself as a Jew first and foremost. Being gay is just a small part of who I am. You know how I figured out I was gay? I knew I was weird; I knew something was going on inside of me. Then my Hebrew school went to see the Israeli Day parade and as we walked down Fifth Avenue, a woman standing on the corner was holding up a sign with the words "My son was homosexual and he went to see Dr. So-and-So and now he's not." And I thought to myself, Oh my God, I have to write that phone number down. That's when I realized that I was gay.

My show is about coming to terms with this whole Jew-gay conflict and being a comic and a mother. I feel like I try to be as traditional as possible, but yet it seems like I don't really fit in anywhere! The truth is that being a Jew is *all* of who I am. It's what I eat, it's how I look, it's how I think, it's my hair, it's my nose, it's everything about me. Being gay is about who I love.

YOUR FAMILY IS ACCEPTING OF WHO YOU ARE?

Yes, now they are. At first they just didn't talk about it. That was the thing—don't talk about it, ignore it and maybe it will go away. But then once I became a mother, my mother couldn't really ignore what was going on. My CD is called *Judith's Roommate Had a Baby* because when Henry was born (my ex gave birth to Henry and I adopted him), my mother didn't know how to explain it, so she would say, "Uh, Judith's roommate had a baby."

I LOVE THAT. THEN YOU HAD THE SECOND CHILD.

I had the second child, but I didn't want to separate them, so after we broke up I got my ex an apartment in the building so I could see them everyday, even if they were sleeping at her place. And she has a girlfriend. My life is a sitcom.

My kids are the most important part of my life. Oh my God, I love love love them. And you know, it's so weird, I hated Hebrew school and they like Hebrew school. It's different now. I think Jews look at things in different ways. I mean, that's the rabbi's job, to interpret these old texts and apply their meanings to our lives—to teach. We have these rabbis who study the same Talmud that the rabbis studied thousands of years ago. It's unbelievable to me.

THE EXPRESSION GOES, "TODAY I AM A MAN." WHAT DID YOU FEEL ON THAT DAY? "TODAY I AM A WO-MAN?"

I felt like a man. I felt like my prostate was enlarged. I felt like my PSA count was high that day. My voice got a little deeper. My balls dropped. It was really weird.

Gene Shalit

For more than thirty-five years, Gene Shalit has been a regular presence on NBC's *Today,* the longest continuous run by one person on a daily network TV program.

He has been reviewing motion pictures, plays and books on television, radio and in major magazines for forty-one years.

His film reviews were a regular feature in *Look* magazine. He wrote the *What's Happening* page for the *Ladies' Home Journal* for twelve years. For a dozen years he wrote and broadcast a daily essay as *Man About Anything* on NBC's coast-to-coast radio network. Shalit was carried on more stations than was any other NBC network radio feature.

He has been a regular panelist on *What's My Line?* and *To Tell the Truth,* and has written articles for the *New York Times, Glamour, TV Guide, Seventeen, McCall's,* and *Cosmopolitan.*

Shalit has performed with the Boston Symphony Orchestra in Boston's Symphony Hall and Tanglewood, played his bassoon on stage in Lincoln Center, and conducted the Pittsburgh Symphony Orchestra in a full concert of classical music. In none of these venues has he ever been invited back.

For national magazines and *Today,* he has interviewed scores of prominent personages in music, theater, and motion pictures, from the Grateful Dead to Sir James Galway to Steven Spielberg to Jessica Lange to Isaac Stern to Luciano Pavarotti to Helen Hayes to Benny Goodman to Mstislav Rostropovich to Sophia Loren to Sophia Loren to Sophia Loren.

Shalit's critically acclaimed anthology of humor, *Laughing Matters* (Doubleday, 1987) was a bestseller. His *Great Hollywood Wit* (St. Martin's Press) appeared in 2002.

Shalit was born in a New York hospital ever so long ago, and eight days later cut out for Newark, New Jersey, to be with his mother. Six years later (1932, for the mathematically challenged) he fled to Morristown, New Jersey, where he later became humor columnist for the high school paper and narrowly escaped expulsion.

Shalit was graduated from the University of Illinois, where he needed only six years to complete his four-year course. While an undergraduate, he was sports editor and humor columnist of the university's daily broadsheet newspaper, *The Daily Illini,* "The World's Greatest College Daily," a columnist for the Twin Cities' *Champaign-Urbana Courier,* and was a Big Ten sports stringer for the Associated Press.

During major league baseball spring training in St. Petersburg, Florida, in 1994, Shalit was run over by a car. To the consternation of scores of Hollywood producers, he recovered.

GENE SHALIT
THE CRITIC'S CHOICE

I don't remember how old I was when I had my bar mitzvah, but it must have been around the time my father, Isadore Shalit, the Elder of the Learned Men of Morristown, New Jersey, said, "It occurs to me that our son is about to be, or at least is approaching the time when, according to the sages, a caterer needs to be chosen. Attention must be paid, and not only attention, but also a rabbi, a cantor, and a yarmulke purveyor, emphasis on the *vey.*"

Thus it came to pass that I was told about a bar mitzvah, which I had assumed was a ranch in Israel.

It was fortuitous that the Pine Brook synagogue was available for the fabled ceremony because my father had sputtered, "I wouldn't set foot in the *farshlogunah* Morristown shul if you paid me!"

So my ceremony was moved thirteen miles to Pine Brook, one minute away the way my father drove.

The bar mitzvah (I was informed) signifies that the boy is now a Man and must from now on adhere to the Ten Commandments. Before that, he was on his own. Thus, too late did I discover that when I was nine I could have coveted my neighbor's wife or made graven images if I had known what graven images were. My neighbor's wife I knew.

Under the rules and regulations of bar mitzvahs, the Jews choose up sides, with the victim and his family on one side and guests (or "gift bearers") on the other.

Arrives the agreed-upon Saturday morning, the innocent lad is led to the altar, where he must singsong a portion of the service called the haftarah in Hebrew if he knows what's good for him.

This I memorized by rote (having no idea what the sounds meant) in the home of my teacher, Cantor Goldberg, every day after school, while hearing my friends outside happily yelling and playing Kick the Can.

What kept me going was my fantasy about what the Hebrew meant, often along the lines of "You will get good presents even from Aunt Bertha and not socks like when you were twelve, amen." The cantor also worked at Drill's Live Chicken Market on Speedwell Avenue, where he grabbed screaming chickens from their cages for customers and slit their throats (the chickens') to render them kosher and deceased. He then tore out most of the feathers, leaving but a short stubble, which my mother (if it was her chicken) removed by burning them off over the gas stove, resulting in a smell that I never again smelled until my dentist, Dr. Glanville, attacked my teeth with an old drill (no relation to Old Man Drill, who owned the chicken store), reproducing that nauseating aroma.

Cantor Goldberg, a man with a bedraggled beard, took my forefinger and touched it to each word as I memorized it (simultaneously forgetting the previous word). To this day I can recall only the very first words. Phonetically they sound like *"Ahm zoo, toe zar tee lee, t'hee law see yo zah pay roo."* The last time I heard Bob Dylan sing one of his songs the lyrics sounded exactly like that. But at the time, Dylan had not been born and his name (when he *was* born) was Zimmerman, not Dylan, which he glommed off the Welsh poet.

Memorization is not my long suit and I had only recently been allowed to wear a long suit as my old-world parents were short-pants-for-children traditionalists, not like today when even two-year-olds get into slacks directly from diapers, whereas the progression of my personal attire was diapers, short pants, knickers, dark blue bar mitzvah suit with two pairs of pants.

The great day dawned bright and clear. I remember Pine Brook flooded by all of my relatives from Brooklyn, disoriented by the absence of sirens and screeching brakes, fearing they were on some overgrown planet and my cousins saying in disbelief, "You live here in the *winter*? What do you *do*?"

On that Saturday morning Americans by the millions across the country set out for work and made sudden U-turns when they realized it was Saturday morning, the Jewish day of rest (except for me), and although they were for the most part Christian, they said if Jews don't have to go to the office today we're not going either. On the other hand, there I was up at the altar in a suit with jacket too loose (which I was afraid my bowels would soon be also), in front of a congregation that included all of my pals I knew were hoping I would forget the words and be embarrassed and they'd razz me.

Then the rabbi pinched my back and it was my turn and I must have navigated the Hebraic rapids successfully, for no thunderbolt crashed upon me and my mother and father stared in relief.

Later, at the sweet table of tea and wine and yellow sponge cake set up in the aromatic gym, I was cluckingly reprimanded by uncles and aunts who said they had never before been to a bar mitzvah where the boy had not made a speech or in some way publicly thanked his parents.

Never mind my not making a speech. Enough I had agreed to wear a tie.

That night back in Morristown when we opened the gifts I remember three fountain pens, some five-dollar bills, one ten, a pair of binoculars, a Monopoly game, a deck of pinochle cards and from Aunt Bertha two pairs of socks. Brown with maroon dots.

I kept the pens, the binoculars and Monopoly. I lost the money playing pinochle. But the next day none of us could figure out what had happened to the socks.

Ronald Perelman

Billionaire businessman and philanthropist, Ronald Owen Perelman was born to be in the boardroom. When he was an eleven-year-old boy, he was attending board meetings for Belmont Industries, a sheet-metal manufacturing plant owned by his father. Two years later he was bar mitzvahed at thirteen and became a man. He graduated from the University of Pennsylvania in 1965 and earned his MBA from the Wharton School in 1966 and joined Belmont Industries, where he stayed until the late 1970s. In 1978 Ronald Perelman began building his empire. He was thirty-five at the time and had wanted to be president of Belmont Industries, but his father disagreed and kept his presidential post.

In 1979, Perelman bought Cohen Hatfield Industries, a jewelry business, and then acquired MacAndrews & Forbes, which became the name of Perelman's holding company. Ronald Perelman continued to buy disparate companies: Marvel Entertainment, Golden State Bank Corp., the Coleman Company and Consolidated Cigar Holdings.

He is now chairman and chief executive officer of MacAndrews & Forbes Holdings Inc. In the corporation's portfolio are some of the most successful companies in their individual lines of business: Revlon, Panavision Inc., AlliedBarton Security Services, AM General, TransTech Pharma, Inc.; Scientific Games Corporation, Deluxe Film, and Clarke American Corp.

Ronald Perelman has interests outside of the business world. As a philanthropist who combines personal resolve and financial resources to get results, he founded Revlon/ UCLA Women's Cancer Research Program, which focuses on breast and ovarian cancer. The program initiated the development of Herceptin, a genetically based cancer treatment and the first of its kind to be approved by the U.S. Food and Drug Administration.

Skin diseases are researched at the Ronald O. Perelman Department of Dermatology at the New York University Medical Center, and patients are given the highest quality of care. Perelman is a board member of Carnegie Hall, the University of Pennsylvania, New York University Medical Center, and he is a member of the French Legion of Honor.

Ronald Perelman lives in New York City and is the father of six children.

RONALD PERELMAN, BILLION DOLLAR BABY

I was bar mitzvahed in a small Conservative synagogue in Philadelphia. I hope this doesn't sound really boring, but my bar mitzvah was probably the most important element of my early years. It was important religious training for me. I grew to really enjoy the lessons and became very close to my teacher. He soon passed away, but he was a very religious man, and very smart. He had this enormous impact on me. I'm Orthodox now, but I grew up in a Conservative family. My bar mitzvah was December 31st, which was a day away from my birthday. I was born January 1st. So we had this terrific New Year's Eve/bar mitzvah party on Saturday night, December 31st. There were about two hundred fifty people there—relatives, my friends and my parents' friends. It was billed as my becoming a man and that's how I thought of it. From that moment on I felt more responsibility for being a Jew.

But my real move toward my religion occurred a few years later, when I was in Israel. It had a dramatic impact on me, and I remember it well. It was when I was in Israel with my family that I became very conscious of being a Jew—much more so than after my bar mitzvah—and I wanted to raise my family in a more traditional lifestyle. I was only eighteen at the time, but I was married when I was twenty. We got married young back then, you know, back in the old days of the covered wagon. After that I became more aware of being more observant and kosher, and more aware of how I wanted to train my kids in their Jewish background. But the foundation of my beliefs was laid by my bar mitzvah teacher. So it had a profound effect on me.

WHAT WAS THE PROCESS LIKE, PREPARING FOR YOUR BIG DAY?

It wasn't bad. Back then we all had records. The cantor would make a recording of your part, and over the summer and all through the year you'd listen to this recording and sing along with it. That's how we learned. My singing voice was not very good. It's improved since then, but it was not very good.

TELL ME ABOUT YOUR OTHER VIVID MEMORIES OF THAT TIME.

I remember that my bar mitzvah party was a lot of fun. There were a lot of kids there and they all had fun. I'm not friendly with any of them anymore, which is sort of sad. The one who was my closest friend, probably through ninth grade, and next to me in all the pictures, was this boy named Gene. And about fifteen years ago I get this little one-page note, "Dear Mr. Perelman, Are you the Ron Perelman that grew up in Elkins Park, Pennsylvania?" Signed "Gene." So I said to my sister, "This is the greatest thing, I found my buddy Gene this week." So, I write back this letter. "Yes, I'm that guy. Tell me what you've been doing." He writes me a four-page letter. "Dear Ronald, I'm now in a Miami correctional institution." The letter went on and on and on. I think he wanted me to get him out of jail. So I tossed that in the wastebasket and never reached out. I haven't seen my friend Gene again. But I've got his pictures all over my bar mitzvah album.

YOU'RE KNOWN TO BE A VERY CONFIDENT, POWERFUL GUY. DID YOU POSSESS THESE QUALITIES BACK THEN?

At thirteen years old you just want to get through it. You just want to finish up and get through it. I mean, you're twelve or thirteen years old. I think I didn't come into my stride until after college, between college and graduate school. But I was competitive in my little world. I didn't think beyond my little world and looking back, I wasn't the most popular kid in the class but I was reasonably popular. I remember something that happened in, I think, ninth grade. I called up this girl named Ellen Friedman, who was a very popular girl in my school. And I said to her, "This is Ronnie. I'd like you to come to the dance with me next Friday night." And she said, "Great." And started talking and talking and talking for about five minutes. And then she says, "Is this Ron Shapiro?" I said, "No. This is Ronnie Perelman." She says, "Oh, I'm busy." I learned a lot from that. You pick yourself up and you go on to the next girl.

I think it's terrible. My daughter Samantha's party was a nice party, a fun party, but a simple party. And that's what I would expect my daughter Caleigh's to be. In other words, nothing elaborate about it. There was no spectacular anything. There was no big-name entertainment. It was not an over-the-top party. And they really do get over the top. I mean the themes and the activities. I think that's just silly and takes away from the meaning. This is something to celebrate, and it's something that clearly should be a memorable activity, but I don't think it should be so outlandish that it's in bad taste. These days, I think that is done too often. In a lot of communities, particularly in the sub-urbs, this is a great status symbol. Who can give the biggest and the most expensive and be the most extraordinary? It's a shame that it does sometimes overshadow the religious experience. But they get religious experience along with it, so I guess that's better than nothing.

CONSIDERING YOU'RE ORTHODOX, WHAT IMPACT DOES RELIGION PLAY IN YOUR EVERYDAY LIFE?

For me, religion is very important. I believe that we don't get to where we are on our own. Part of it is through our efforts. Part of it is where we're put to achieve those results. Every morning I talk to a rabbi whom I've known for forty-five years in Philadelphia. Every day, we go over the Torah portion for that day in a short time, around five minutes. I call him, no matter where I am in the world. And then once a week we'll meet and have a more ex-panded conversation. This is very important to me. And I think it's good for my kids to see this, so it will be important to them, too. So I think it's more about understanding or ac-cepting—your role and your activities, and the impact and lack of impact that that has brought about the results. There's also an obligation to give back to those who are less fortu-nate than you. So every Saturday I go to synagogue and when I get called before the Torah, it has that same sort of impact as my bar mitzvah. A bar mitzvah can happen at different times. I once had an assistant, a red-headed Irish kid named Durnam. And after about three years with me, he told me that his mother was not Irish. She was Jewish. Of course, that makes him Jewish in the eyes of the Jewish religion. He had never been bar mitzvahed. So, on one of my trips, when we had a minyan, he got bar mitzvahed. This had an enormous effect on his life. He now is a Jew. He always knew that he had a Jewish mother, but he never connected the dots. It meant a lot to me to be able to do this for him.

Senator Joseph Lieberman

Senator Joseph Lieberman has never shied away from making commitments. From doing the best job he could as a bar mitzvah boy, to his astounding accomplishments as a United States senator, Lieberman has given our country his spirit, drive and ability to make our home a better place. His involvement in public policy is as close to endless as humanly possible.

A native of Connecticut, Senator Joseph Lieberman has dedicated his life to public service, his family, and his religion. After earning his law degree in 1967, Lieberman was elected in 1970 to the Connecticut State Senate, where he served for ten years. He went into private practice in the early 1980s and then served as Connecticut's twenty-first attorney general until 1988. During this time, Lieberman took on polluters of his state's environment. He also took on deadbeat dads by increasing the enforcement of child support. As a defender of consumers' rights, his fan base grew. His election to the United States Senate in 1988 launched him into a nearly twenty-year career (to date) as a United States senator. In his most recent victory in 2006, Lieberman ran as an Independent, showing his commitment to public service, and as a supporter of Americans, regardless of party.

His stand on security issues has changed the way the United States is protected. He led the Senate into establishing the Department of Homeland Security to ensure that our nation has the best protection possible from terrorist attacks. He advances economic policies that encourage the growth of businesses and markets for American goods and services. He supports public schools and encourages students to achieve. He believes that all Americans should have the opportunity to go to college so that they have

Senator Joseph Lieberman

a better chance at a successful career. Senator Lieberman wants America to be a smart country, and a healthy one. A goal is to make sure that Americans have access to quality health care they can afford. His hope is that Medicare and Social Security will be available for our descendents. His belief in the strength of family is evident by his take on religion, and how it draws families together.

Senator Lieberman is chairman and former ranking member of the Homeland Security and Governmental Affairs Committee. He is a member of the Environment and Public Works Committee where he is the chairman of the Subcommittee on Private Sector and Consumer Solutions to Global Warming and Wildlife Protection; Senate Armed Services Committee, where he is chairman of the Subcommittee on AirLand Forces, and sits on the Personnel and Sea Power Subcommittees; he is also a member of the Small Business Committee.

Senator Lieberman and his wife, Hadassah, live in New Haven, Connecticut, and Washington. They have four children, Matthew, Rebecca, Ethan and Hana, and three granddaughters, Tennessee, Willie, and Eden, and a grandson, Yitzak.

JOSEPH LIEBERMAN
TODAY I AM AN INDEPENDENT

As my youngest child, who is now 18, says, we are a classic 1950s Orthodox family where the rabbi has tremendous influence in one's life. Our rabbi, Rabbi Joseph Ehrenkranz, always preached very outward-reaching Orthodox Judaism. That is, outward-reaching in the community through actions, social action included. I was bar mitzvahed in a synagogue in Stamford, Connecticut. I was born and raised in Stamford. The synagogue, called Agudath Sholom, still exists but now in a different building.

If my mother were still alive, she would remember details of my bar mitzvah. She passed away about a year and a half ago. My dad passed away quite a long time ago. But what I remember is that I'm pretty sure there was a kiddush afterward, downstairs in the social hall. It was not too extravagant. My bar mitzvah had a significant religious component. I worked hard to learn how to lead the service and then to read a part of the Torah. I remember that it was the first time ever that I got up and actually led the service and filled a kind of cantorial role. My grandmother was very proud of what I was doing. She was a very important force in my life. We lived with her in her house for the first eight years of my life. When we moved, she spent at least half of every week with us.

CONSIDERING YOU WERE RAISED ORTHODOX, TELL ME WHAT THE SERVICE AND CELEBRATION MEANT TO YOU AT THE TIME

It was very, very special to me. We had a party at the Jewish Community Center that night. My parents wanted it to be a nice event. There was a kosher caterer in town, who also cooked for the local Jewish Center day camp. Actually, she was my first employer. I think that a year before my bar mitzvah, I went to work for her. Her name was Mrs. Falk. I worked as a waiter for her in the summer before my bar mitzvah. That was the first job I ever had in my life. And the first time I saw how mashed potatoes were made led me not to want to eat mashed potatoes, other than in my own house. I can't tell you that much about the party but there was a pretty good crowd there and we ate good, down-home kosher cooking.

I remember that we had boys and girls at the party. And there was mixed dancing. Like I said, classic 1950s Orthodox. I was pretty active. I hate to call myself popular, but I was always sociable and had a lot of friends. Most of my friends were actually not Jewish. Stamford was a very ethnically diverse, racially diverse community. I had a lot of non-Jewish kids at my bar mitzvah. They were fascinated by it, as I recall, and very respectful. I had a secret crush on a girl named Maddie but in those days, it didn't go much further, at thirteen, than a secret crush.

About the gifts, there was a joke at that time, that "today I am a fountain pen" business, because everybody got fountain pens. I actually got a lot of cuff links. Who ever thought that a thirteen-year-old kid would wear French cuffs? I remember that I did get all the envelopes. And I gave them to my dad, and they put them in a savings account. And they gave it to me later, either when I got out of college, or even possibly when I got married so the amount had grown. It was a classic wonderful parental thing to do.

And I remember that, at least in Stamford at the time, maybe it still happens, we had the climactic candle-lighting ceremony. At the bar mitzvah party, there were, of course, thirteen candles on the cake. Different members of the family were called and honored by

154

being asked to light a candle. So my grandmother, my uncles, my aunts, my sister all lit candles.

My mother and father asked a cousin, who was a high school teacher, to be the master of ceremonies. He claimed for years later, and he lived into his nineties, that as he called on me to light the last candle, the thirteenth candle, he predicted that I would one day be a United States senator. His name was Abe Hecht and if only he were alive, he could tell you stories.

THAT'S INCREDIBLE! HE COULD HAVE PREDICTED THAT YOU WOULD BE A DOCTOR OR A LAWYER. WHY DO YOU THINK HE SAID A SENATOR?

I don't know. And it's too bad. I kind of remember that he said it, but honestly, what did it mean to me, at that point? Really, what I wanted to be was center fielder for a major-league baseball team.

SO, YOU WERE HOPING HE'D SAY, "TODAY, YOU ARE A MAN, AND WHEN YOU ARE A MAN FOR REAL, YOU WILL BE A BASEBALL PLAYER." *NOT* . . . "WHEN YOU GROW UP, YOU'LL BE A SENA-TOR."

A senator, what the heck is that? Anyway, that's what I remember. There were a lot of kids, my parents were very generous that way, and a lot of family and my parents' friends. There could have been one hundred and fifty in that hall. But it wasn't extravagant. I remember my mom joking with me some years ago about how much it cost them, because it was nothing by today's standards. What did Mrs. Falk charge for a meal? $5, $7.50? I don't know. And it was in the JCC auditorium, not in a big hotel or anything. And the synagogue itself, which now has a beautiful social hall, didn't have much of a social hall, then.

DID YOU HAVE ANY SORT OF FEELING WHEN YOU WERE UP THERE THAT YOU WOULD ONE DAY BE IN THE PUBLIC EYE?

That's really interesting. I probably was on some kind of track to try to accomplish something. But I don't know how defined it was. I mean, I did well at school. I wanted to do well as I said, to learn the various parts of the service, to lead them all, and then to read from the Torah, and to give a speech.

I had a sort of confidence and pride about it, and needless to say, I was showered with praise from my parents. I will share this story that I love to tell. It happened later, but it'll give you a flavor and idea of my upbringing. A very close friend came from Yale to my home in Stamford for a weekend. And on the way back, he said to me, "You know, your parents are just so supportive and proud of you." He said, "I have this picture in my mind that when you were a kid, and you would come down for breakfast in the morning, your parents would give you a standing ovation."

In reality, it wasn't quite that way. But they were very supportive in a loving, demanding way. And that is an incredible gift in life. It's probably just about the best thing that can happen to a person early in life, to have parents who believe in them and encourage them. I think that played out at the bar mitzvah because I felt that I was expected to stretch and do all the parts of the service, and to give a good speech.

GETTING BACK TO WHAT YOUR FRIEND SAID, DID YOU AT LEAST GET A STANDING OVATION FROM YOUR PARENTS AT YOUR BAR MITZVAH?

No. But I got a lot of praise. And of course, when I got called to light the thirteenth candle, and an introduction as a future senator, I got quite a round of applause.

CLEARLY, JUDAISM IS VITAL TO YOUR WHOLE FAMILY. IN FACT, YOUR SON IS A RABBI?

He's my stepson and, yes, he is. So, I don't want to take total genetic credit for that. My other son is a principal of a Jewish day school in Atlanta. All of the kids are involved in Jewish life. It's fascinating. Two of my kids have gone to law school but the one who's the principal of the Jewish day school in Atlanta just didn't enjoy law practice, went into teaching and loved it, and then applied around the country to be a principal and ended up in Atlanta. My daughter went to law school, and has worked in human service and charitable organizations. Now she consults for Jewish foundations, so she's mostly involved in an Israeli-based foundation.

HOW DO YOU FEEL ABOUT TODAY'S MORE EXTRAVAGANT BAR MITZVAH CELEBRATIONS THAT ARE MORE ABOUT THE PARTY THAN THE SERVICE?

If your family has the capacity, and they really want to throw a big party, they can do that. But then you've got to work a little harder to make sure that the kids understand what they're stepping into. Because it's a rite of passage, it's the moment when you're deemed to be of age, and therefore responsible to try to conduct yourself according to the principles and practices of the religion. And also, in a larger sense, to accept the torch of Jewish history and Jewish destiny, that goes back, by our count, six millennia, and to carry it forward. So it's quite a moment. And I think it's important for that not to get lost in the big party. There are too many jokes about the fact that the bar mitzvah becomes, too often, a graduation from Hebrew school, instead of what it's really meant to be, which is the moment when you're respected as an adult and you also take on responsibilities.

YOUR RELIGION HAS BEEN SUCH AN IMPORTANT PART OF YOUR LIFE. HOW DOES IT PLAY IN TO YOUR LIFE NOW, WITH THIS KEY POSITION YOU HOLD?

For a while, I stopped observing the Sabbath, but then I came back to it shortly after I got married and had children. It's such an important part of my life, and sometimes people say to me—how can you be involved in campaigns and how can you be a senator and still keep the Sabbath? And the answer is, "How could I do it without keeping the Sabbath?" Because the Sabbath is a time to stop, a time to to be reflective. It's a time to be with your family. It's a time to not have the pressures of the rest of the week, to appreciate what you've been given, and the opportunities you have.

But there's no question that we're all the result of what has gone before, our life experience, our parents, our reading of history. And there's no question to me, that part of me, who votes on matters or takes positions, has been greatly affected by the sum total of Jewish history, ethics, and social values. So it's very much a part of me. And it continues. The more I go out in life, the more I'm grateful for, and grateful to my parents for putting me on this path. To me this is a source of great strength.

PHOTO CREDITS

Page 2, courtesy of Jill Rappaport

Pages 5, 8, 16, 26, 36, 42, 48, 57, 62, 68, 71, 76, 78, 85, 90, 103, 107, 110, 118, 124, 127 (matchbook), 130, 146, and 152, courtesy of Linda Solomon

Pages 9, 11, and 13, courtesy of Joyce Piven

Pages 17, 19, and 23, courtesy of Michael Kors

Pages 27, 28, 31, and 34, courtesy of Harvey Fierstein

Page 43, courtesy of Jeff Zucker

Page 49, courtesy of Noah Wyle

Page 63, courtesy of Charles Grodin

Page 69, 70, 72, 73, courtesy of Donny Deutsch

Page 77, courtesy of Richard Dreyfuss

Page 84, courtesy of Howie Mandel

Page 91, 98, courtesy of Andy and Josh Bernstein

Page 102, courtesy of Marlee Matlin

Page 111, 112, 115, courtesy of Henry Winkler

Page 119, courtesy of Ed Koch

Page 125, 127 (tables, cake), courtesy of Ruth Bell

Page 131, courtesy of Judy Gold

Page 140, 141, courtesy of Gene Shalit

Page 147, courtesy of Ronald Perelman